A COURSE IN PERSONAL DISCIPLESHIP TO STRENGTHEN YOUR WALK WITH GOD

BEARING FRUIT
IN GOD'S FAMILY

THE NEW
2:7 SERIES

NAVPRESS

NAVPRESS ◑

NavPress is the publishing ministry of The Navigators, an international Christian organization and leader in personal spiritual development. NavPress is committed to helping people grow spiritually and enjoy lives of meaning and hope through personal and group resources that are biblically rooted, culturally relevant, and highly practical.

For a free catalog go to www.NavPress.com
or call 1.800.366.7788 in the United States or 1.800.839.4769 in Canada.

The Navigators' Church Discipleship Ministry (CDM) is focused on helping churches become more intentional in disciplemaking. CDM staff nationwide are available to help church leadership develop the critical components that will enable them to accomplish Christ's Great Commission. For further information on how CDM can help you, E-mail us at cdm@navigators.org, or visit our web site: www.navigators.org/cdm.

ISBN 978-1-57683-192-2

Important

PARTICIPANTS

This course is designed to be used *only* by those who have successfully completed *Growing Strong in God's Family* and *Deepening Your Roots in God's Family*. These books are available from your Christian Bookstore, NavPress, or a local Navigator staff person.

GROUP LEADERSHIP

It is important for one person to act as the leader during each group meeting. This may be the same person each time, or the responsibility may be shared by two or three group members.

LEADER TRAINING

Excellent leader training seminars are available once or twice a year in many areas of the United States, Canada, and several other countries. Those who attend a leader training seminar learn how to maximize the effectiveness of *Bearing Fruit in God's Family* and the other two books in *The New 2:7 Series*.

Information about training seminars may be obtained from: Church Discipleship Ministry, The Navigators, P.O. Box 6000, Colorado Springs, CO 80934. E-mail: cdm@navigators.org, or web site: www.navigators.org/cdm.

In Canada, contact The Navigators of Canada Resource Centre, 490 Dutton Drive, Unit B-12, Waterloo, Ontario, N21 6H7. Phone/Fax: 1-800-839-4769, web site: www/navigators.ca.

LEADER'S GUIDE

A detailed Leader's Guide for *Bearing Fruit in God's Family* can be downloaded from the Church Discipleship Ministry web site at **www.navigators.org/cdm**. Suggestions in the Leader's Guide are clear, specific, and practical. You will want a copy of the Leader's Guide before you lead others through Book 3.

ACKNOWLEDGMENT

We are grateful for the dedicated efforts of Ron Oertli who originated the concept of *The 2:7 Series* and is its principal author.

Contents

COMPLETION RECORD   7

SESSION 1   9
    Review the Goals of Book 2   9
    Scripture Memory Instructions—Week One   10
    The *Topical Memory System* in This Book   11
    How to Meditate on the Scriptures—Part 1   13
    Openly Identifying with Christ   18

SESSION 2   20
    Scripture Memory Instructions—Week Two   20
    How to Meditate on the Scriptures—Part 2   21
    Introduction to Bible Study—Book 3   23

SESSION 3   25
    Scripture Memory Instructions—Week Three   25
    Bible Study—"The Call to Fruitful Living"   26

SESSION 4   34
    Scripture Memory Instructions—Week Four   34
    "Relationship Evangelism Bible Study"   35

SESSION 5   39
    Scripture Memory Instructions—Week Five   39
    Bible Study—"Love in Action"   40

SESSION 6   46
    Scripture Memory Instructions—Week Six   46
    Bible Study—"Purity of Life"   47

SESSION 7   54
    Scripture Memory Instructions—Week Seven   54
    The Bridge Illustration   55

SESSION 8   66

    Bible Study — "Integrity in Living"   66

SESSION 9   72

    Verse Analysis of Matthew 6:33   72

    Priorities — Part 1   76

SESSION 10   81

    Priorities — Part 2   81

SESSION 11   87

    Bible Study — "Character in Action"   87

    Keep On Keeping On   93

NOTES   95

Bible Reading Highlights Record and Prayer Sheets are included following page 96.

Completion Record

Ask others in your study group to check you on your completion of the requirements in this course and have them initial and date each section.

SCRIPTURE MEMORY	Initial	Date
Proclaim Christ, TMS B 1-12, memory verses:		
Required verses:		
"All Have Sinned"—Romans 3:23		
"Sin's Penalty"—Romans 6:23		
"Christ Paid the Penalty"—Romans 5:8		
"Salvation Not by Works"—Ephesians 2:8-9		
"Must Receive Christ"—John 1:12		
"Assurance of Salvation"—1 John 5:13		
Optional verses:		
"All Have Sinned"—Isaiah 53:6		
"Sin's Penalty"—Hebrews 9:27		
"Christ Paid the Penalty"—1 Peter 3:18		
"Salvation Not by Works"—Titus 3:5		
"Must Receive Christ"—Romans 10:9-10		
"Assurance of Salvation"—John 5:24		
Quoted the six required verses, *Proclaim Christ*, B-1,3,5,7,9,11		
Reviewed all of *Live the New Life,* A 1-6 (and the optional 7-12 if applicable) for 14 consecutive days		
Reviewed all of *Beginning with Christ* for 14 consecutive days		
QUIET TIME		
Completed *Bible Reading Highlights Record* for 14 consecutive days		
EVANGELISM		
Identified with Christ in a relating activity (page 18)		
Completed "Relationship Evangelism Bible Study" (pages 35-38)		

Testimony given with or without notes in less than 4 minutes		
Used Evangelism Prayer List for 7 consecutive days		
Gave *The Bridge Illustration:*		
Outline		
"Lecture" presentation 1		
"Lecture" presentation 2		
BIBLE STUDY		
Session 3—"The Call to Fruitful Living" (pages 26-33)		
Session 5—"Love in Action" (pages 40-45)		
Session 6—"Purity of Life" (pages 47-53)		
Session 8—"Integrity in Living" (pages 66-71)		
Session 11—"Character in Action" (pages 87-93)		
OTHER		
Meditation exercise (pages 13-17)		
Completed Matthew 6:33 study (pages 72-75)		
Completed "Priorities—Part 1" (pages 76-80)		
Studied "Priorities—Part 2" (pages 81-86)		
LEADER'S CHECK		
Graduated from Book 3		

SESSION 1

OUTLINE OF THIS SESSION:
1. Go over "Review the Goals of Book 2" (page 9).
2. Preview Book 3 by looking over the *Completion Record* (pages 7-8).
3. Survey the "Scripture Memory Instructions—Week One" (pages 10-11).
4. Read "The Topical Memory System in This Book" (pages 11-13).
5. Complete "How to Meditate on the Scriptures—Part 1"(pages 13-17).
   a. Write out a paraphrase of 2 Timothy 3:16.
   b. Ask yourself questions on Hebrews 10:24-25.
6. Discuss current use of the Evangelism Prayer List.
7. Read and discuss "Openly Identifying with Christ" (page 18).
8. Read the "Assignment for Session 2" (page 19).
9. Close the session in prayer.

Review the Goals of Book 2

The goals of Book 2 were:
1. To experience a more consistent and meaningful quiet time by . . .
   a. combining meaningful Bible reading and prayer.
   b. succeeding in having 14 consecutive quiet times during the course.
   c. recording daily quiet time thoughts and how they impressed you on a *Bible Reading Highlights Record.*
   d. growing in your ability to share key quiet time thoughts with others in the group.
2. To quote accurately the five Scripture memory verses of *Beginning with Christ* (the five Assurance verses).
3. To memorize at least six verses of the *Topical Memory System* successfully. (These six verses are correlated with *The Wheel Illustration.*)
4. To study and discuss the booklet *My Heart Christ's Home.*
5. To have a half day of prayer after reading and discussing the article *How to Spend a Day in Prayer.*

6. To complete and discuss five studies as a participant in a Bible study group.
7. To give a personal salvation testimony in less than four minutes, using notes from a 3 x 5 card.
8. To relate with a nonChristian friend through a nonspiritual activity.

Scripture Memory Instructions — Week One
From The Navigators' *Topical Memory System*

You're Under Way . . .

You're off to a good start, having completed at least half of the first unit of the *Topical Memory System* (A 1-12) in Book 2.

You have begun to enjoy some of the benefits Scripture memory can bring. Now keep up your momentum as you tackle six of the next 12 verses (B 1-12).

Study these instructions, then each week read the comments *About the Verses* and follow the instructions in the section *Your Weekly Plan.*

Continue to Write the Verses on 3 x 5 Cards

During this course you will continue to put your memory verses on 3 x 5 cards. Write out, type, or computer print the Scripture passage on one side. On the other side put the topic and reference.

What to Expect

Scripture memory can help us in three major areas—witnessing effectively, overcoming anxiety, and having victory over temptation. In Book 3 you will learn at least six verses which will greatly contribute to your effectiveness in witnessing.

Use the Buddy System

The Scriptures teach that "as iron sharpens iron, so one man sharpens another" (Proverbs 27:17), and "Two are other" (Proverbs 27:17), and "Two are

better than one . . . If one falls down, his friend can help him up" (Ecclesiastes 4:9-10). We all need encouragement in our Christian lives and this surely applies to memorizing Scripture.

Ask someone else in your 2:7 group to get together with you outside class to help you review your verses. You may also want to talk over any difficulties you are having, but *above all, share how God is using the verses in your lives.* This will help you succeed in Scripture memory.

Knowledge and Application

Some Christians confuse Bible knowledge with spiritual maturity, assuming that knowing more about the Bible automatically makes a person a better Christian. This is not necessarily true. The Pharisees knew the Old Testament, yet they were spiritually blind. The key to spiritual maturity is sincere application of God's Word to life.

The apostle Paul addressed the Corinthian believers as fleshly, unspiritual babes in Christ. He had to feed them milk instead of solid spiritual food. They took pride in wisdom and logic, and could have understood the deeper truths Paul wanted to impart to them. But their lives contradicted what they professed to believe. Jealousy and strife split their ranks, and they behaved like ordinary, unregenerate people. Their lives were too much like those of the unbelievers in Corinth. What an indictment! They needed to apply the Word of God to their daily living.

Visualize the Verse

We remember pictures more easily than words or concepts. If you find it difficult to connect a particular verse with its topic and reference, try forming a mental picture of the verse based on its content, context, or some other feature that will help you remember. The picture can become the mental hook you use later to draw the verse from your memory. It helps if you make the image as unusual or striking as possible.

For example, consider the verses in Book 2 on witnessing, Matthew 4:19 and Romans 1:16. Associate the first verse with Christ and the second with Paul. Picture Jesus standing on a beach by the Sea of Galilee. Two fishermen are tending their nets when He calls out, "Come, follow me, and I will make you fishers of men." Fix this scene in your mind. Associate the picture with the topic of witnessing and with the reference Matthew 4:19.

Paul didn't write the book of Romans from Rome, but because it was addressed to the believers there, you might picture Paul standing in the Roman Forum or Coliseum speaking out to the pagan citizens, "I am not ashamed of the gospel because it is the power of God for the salvation of everyone who believes: first for the Jew, then for the Gentile." Associate this picture with the topic of witnessing and with the reference Romans 1:16.

Visualizing a verse is especially helpful if you find it difficult to remember by ordinary means.

The Topical Memory System *in This Book*

You have already learned at least half of the first 12 verses in the *Topical Memory System*, a series of verses called **A**. *Live the New Life*. The four remaining series are **B**. *Proclaim Christ*; **C**. *Be Christ's Disciple*; **D**. *Grow in Christlikeness*; and **E**. *Rely on God's Resources*.

During this course you will memorize the first six verses from B. *Proclaim Christ*. These are key verses you can use for explaining the gospel to others. It is optional as to whether you memorize more than six verses.

B. *Proclaim Christ*	Required:	Optional:
All Have Sinned	Romans 3:23	Isaiah 53:6
Sin's Penalty	Romans 6:23	Hebrews 9:27
Christ Paid the Penalty	Romans 5:8	1 Peter 3:18
Salvation Not by Works	Ephesians 2:8-9	Titus 3:5
Must Receive Christ	John 1:12	Romans 10:9-10
Assurance of Salvation	1 John 5:13	John 5:24

Below are the topics and references for both the required and optional verses from Books 1 and 2. Plan to end Book 3 with the ability to skillfully quote all the verses you have memorized during *The New 2:7 Series*. By the end of this course you will have memorized at least 17 verses! That's great! You will have those verses readily available for recall to apply to your own life or to use in helping others. Plan to keep those verses sharp for a lifetime!

From *Beginning with Christ:*	Required:
Assurance of Salvation	1 John 5:11-12
Assurance of Answered Prayer	John 16:24
Assurance of Victory	1 Corinthians 10:13
Assurance of Forgiveness	1 John 1:9
Assurance of Guidance	Proverbs 3:5-6

A. *Live the New Life*	Required:	Optional:
Christ the Center	2 Corinthians 5:17	Galatians 2:20
Obedience to Christ	Romans 12:1	John 14:21
The Word	2 Timothy 3:16	Joshua 1:8
Prayer	John 15:7	Philippians 4:6-7
Fellowship	1 John 1:3	Hebrews 10:24-25
Witnessing	Matthew 4:19	Romans 1:16

MEDITATION—AN AID TO APPLICATION

One of the most beneficial reasons for memorizing Scripture verses is that it stimulates us to meditate on their contents. During this course you will be doing an exercise (pages 13-17) to increase your ability to meditate on passages of Scripture.

An important part of your Scripture memory program should be meditating on verses you have learned. Not only will this enable you to retain them in your memory with accuracy, but as you reflect on and consider their contents, you will experience challenges, encouragement, and motivation. Remember God's instruction to Joshua: "Do not let this Book of the law depart from your mouth; meditate on it day and night, so that you may be careful to do everything written in it. Then you will be prosperous and successful" (Joshua 1:8).

IMPORTANCE OF DAILY REVIEW

Continual review is the key to having a grasp on the verses you already have learned. An excellent goal you could establish would be to know your memory verses so well by the end of Book 3 that you cannot only quote them accurately, but also quickly list the specific topics under Series A and Series B, as well as the *Beginning with Christ* verses. Plan not only to complete your memory assignments each week in Book 3, but also to quote daily the topics and references of all the verses you have learned.

Scripture memory and meditation is a strategic part of the discipleship training in which you are involved. It promotes your spiritual development and lays the foundation for future spiritual growth. You will agree then with the psalmist: "Oh, how I love your law! I meditate on it all day long" (Psalm 119:97).

How to Meditate on the Scriptures—Part 1
A Group Exercise

> *Blessed is the man*
> > *who does not walk in the counsel of the wicked*
> *or stand in the way of sinners*
> > *or sit in the seat of mockers.*
> *But his delight is in the law of the LORD,*
> > *and on his law he meditates day and night.*
> *He is like a tree planted by streams of water,*
> > *which yields its fruit in season*
> *and whose leaf does not wither.*
> > *Whatever he does prospers.*
> > > > > *—Psalm 1:1-3*

WHAT IS MEDITATION?
Meditation is the act of reflecting on, pondering, musing over, or contemplating. Meditation is *not* mind-wandering or indulging in "mental drifting," but it has form and an object. Bible verses and scriptural concepts are the focus of a Christian's meditation.

When we meditate, we spend a few moments *directing* our thoughts to a single subject. Meditation is thinking with a purpose.

Meditation is *not* a solemn, academic exercise. It requires an attitude of curiosity and expectation leading to exciting discoveries, refreshment of spirit, and transformation of character. It brings reward and benefit.

When we meditate, we purposefully sort through information for clarification, for application, for categorization, and for assimilation.

FURTHER INSIGHT INTO MEDITATION
> *This book of the Law must never depart from your mouth; you must meditate on it day and night, so that you may keep living in accord with all that is written in it; for then you will make your way successful, and then you will prosper.*
> > > > *—Joshua 1:8 (BERKELEY)*

During this class session you will have opportunity to practice two methods of meditation on pages 14-17. As part of your homework for next week, you will practice four additional methods of meditation, pages 21-23 — a total of six methods.

1—Paraphrase

The first method of meditation you will practice is to write a paraphrase. As you attempt to put a verse or passage into your own words, you will come to understand it more clearly. Some exciting insights can result from writing your own paraphrase.

On the lines on page 15 write out 2 Timothy 3:16 in your own words, using the translations and paraphrases below to help you complete this part of your work. (You may want to use more words in your paraphrase than are in the original verse.)

VARIOUS TRANSLATIONS AND PARAPHRASES OF 2 TIMOTHY 3:16

"All Scripture is God-breathed and is useful for teaching, rebuking, correcting and training in righteousness."

"All Scripture is given by inspiration of God, and is profitable for doctrine, for reproof, for correction, for instruction in righteousness" (NKJV).

"All Scripture is inspired by God and profitable for teaching, for reproof, for correction, for training in righteousness" (NASB).

"For all Scripture is inspired by God and is useful for teaching the truth, rebuking error, correcting faults, and giving instruction for right living" (TEV).

"All Scripture is inspired by God and profitable for teaching, for reproof, for correction, and for training in righteousness" (RSV).

"All Scripture is inspired by God and can profitably be used for teaching, for refuting error, for guiding people's lives and teaching them to be holy" (JB).

"Every Scripture is God-breathed—given by His inspiration—and profitable for instruction, for reproof and conviction of sin, for correction of error and discipline in obedience, and for training in righteousness [that is, in holy living, in conformity to God's will in thought, purpose, and action]" (AMP).

YOUR PARAPHRASE OF 2 TIMOTHY 3:16

_____
_____
_____
_____
_____
_____
_____
_____
_____
_____
_____
_____
_____
_____
_____
_____
_____
_____
_____
_____
_____
_____
_____
_____

2—Questions

A second method of meditation to practice now is to ask yourself questions about a verse. You may use two possible methods in asking yourself questions. You may use the _who, what, when, where, why,_ and _how_ questions, or you may jot down random questions which come to mind as you reflect on the passage. You may not come up with answers immediately for all of your questions.

On the lines on page 17 jot down some of the questions and answers that come to mind as you meditate on Hebrews 10:24-25, using the translations and paraphrases below to help you. Begin by asking who, what, where, when, why, or how, or use random questions.

VARIOUS TRANSLATIONS AND PARAPHRASES OF HEBREWS 10:24-25

"Let us consider how we may spur one another on toward love and good deeds. Let us not give up meeting together, as some are in the habit of doing, but let us encourage one another—and all the more as you see the Day approaching."

"And let us consider one another in order to stir up love and good works, not forsaking the assembling of ourselves together, as is the manner of some, but exhorting one another, and so much the more as you see the Day approaching." (NKJV).

"And let us consider how to stimulate one another to love and good deeds, not forsaking our own assembling together, as is the habit of some, but encouraging *one another,* and all the more, as you see the day drawing near" (NASB).

"Let us be concerned for one another, to help one another to show love and do good. Let us not give up the habit of meeting together as some are doing. Instead, let us encourage one another all the more, since you see that the Day of the Lord is coming nearer" (TEV).

"And let us consider how to stir up one another to love and good works, not neglecting to meet together, as is the habit of some, but encouraging one another, and all the more as you see the Day drawing near" (RSV).

"Let us be concerned for each other, to stir a response in love and good works. Do not stay away from the meetings of the community, as some do, but encourage each other to go; the more so as you see the Day drawing near" (JB).

"And let us consider *and* give attentive, continuous care to watching over one another, studying how we may stir up (stimulate and incite) to love *and* helpful deeds *and* noble activities; not forsaking or neglecting to assemble together (as believers), as is the habit of some people, but admonishing—warning, urging, and encouraging—one another, and all the more faithfully as you see the day approaching" (AMP).

QUESTIONS ABOUT HEBREWS 10:24-25

MEDITATION EXERCISES IN SESSION 2
In this session you have used two techniques for meditating on the Scriptures: paraphrase and questions. In session 2, "How to Meditate on the Scriptures — Part 2," you will experience four more meditation approaches: prayer, emphasis, cross-reference, and application.

Openly Identifying with Christ

During Book 2 you had an assignment to participate in at least one "non-spiritual" activity with a pre-Christian. Since then you have probably been involved in several activities with one or more pre-Christians. As you know, spending time together is the primary way in which you develop friendship and openness with an individual.

During Book 3 you are required to openly identify with Christ when you are with a pre-Christian acquaintance. Some call this "flying the flag." Old sailing ships flew the flag of their country so that they could be identified from a distance by another ship. They were "flying the flag" of the sovereign and country for whom they held allegiance. There is a point when a Christian needs to verbally begin "flying the flag"—not in a pushy way, but naturally and openly.

To openly identify with Christ does not mean to give your complete testimony or share the gospel. It simply means that you make a statement or comment that identifies you with Christ. It is wise to prepare what you might like to say when you have the opportunity. You could refer to something you heard in a sermon at church or something your child heard in Sunday school. You could refer to something Christ said in one of the gospels. You could make a brief statement about praying for someone or something. Be direct enough to be understood. Be confident, yet gentle. Never sound defensive.

And the Lord's servant must not quarrel; instead, he must be kind to everyone, able to teach, not resentful. Those who oppose him he must gently instruct, in the hope that God will grant them repentance leading them to a knowledge of the truth.

—2 Timothy 2:24-25

It is good to identify with Christ early in a relationship. The longer you go in the relationship without identifying with Christ, the harder it will be to share your faith with that person. Pray for wisdom and boldness, make a plan, then carry it out in a gracious manner.

You may remember the interesting conversation between God and Jeremiah in Jeremiah 1:6-8. Jeremiah spoke first. "'Ah, Sovereign LORD,' I said, 'I do not know how to speak; I am only a child.' But the LORD said to me, 'Do not say, "I am only a child." You must go to everyone I send you to and say whatever I command you. Do not be afraid of them, for I am with you and will rescue you,' declares the LORD." You, too, may sometimes feel fearful or uneasy, but God will give you the courage and wisdom to say what needs to be said. Later you can build on this brief spiritual conversation.

ASSIGNMENT FOR SESSION 2:

1. Scripture Memory: Study and complete "Scripture Memory Instructions—
   Week Two" (pages 20-21). Memorize the verse on "All Have Sinned,"
   Romans 3:23.
2. Quiet Time: Continue your Bible reading, marking, and recording, and using
   your Prayer Sheets.
3. Evangelism: Come to class prepared to give your personal testimony without
   notes in less than four minutes.
4. Other: Complete "How to Meditate on the Scriptures — Part 2" (pages 21-
   23). Meditation should not be hurried; take your time and enjoy the
   exercises.

SESSION 2

OUTLINE OF THIS SESSION:
1. Break into verse review groups and review the verse on "All Have Sinned," Romans 3:23. (Work at getting anything signed that you can on your *Completion Record.*)
2. Share some quiet time thoughts from your *Bible Reading Highlights Record.*
3. Do "How to Meditate on the Scriptures — Part 2" (pages 21-23).
4. Have two or three people give a personal testimony with or without notes in less than four minutes.
5. Read "Introduction to Bible Study—Book 3" (pages 23-24).
6. Read the "Assignment for Session 3" (page 24).
7. Close the session in prayer.

Scripture Memory Instructions—Week Two

And Now to Continue . . .

You have three things to work with each week as you do the new memory verses on the topics of *Proclaim Christ:*

1. *Your Memory Materials*—to use daily. The required memory verses are listed on page 11. On a 3 x 5 card copy the topic and reference on one side. On the other side copy the words of the verse. Decide the translation from which you will memorize. Memorize and review from the 3 x 5 cards.

2. *About the Verses*—to make the verses more meaningful and easier to learn and apply.

3. *Your Weekly Plan*—to help you progress step by step in your memory work and avoid pitfalls.

About the Verses

SERIES B . PROCLAIM CHRIST

As witnesses for Jesus Christ we have two things to share—*our testimony* of how we found Christ and what He means to us now, and *the gospel*, God's plan of salvation. The gospel explains the deep need of all people, God's love for every individual, and Christ's death on the cross to make eternal life possible.

The topics and verses in this series form a usable outline for presenting the gospel. They will help you become more skillful in proclaiming Christ.

TOPIC 1. ALL HAVE SINNED

Today's complex world presents seemingly insurmountable problems of war, crime, racial strife, and violence of all kinds. Experts search desperately for solutions, but few acknowledge the basic cause. Christ, however, went to the root of the matter. He said that envy, pride, impurity, immorality, theft, murder, and wickedness are merely results of the real problem—our sinful hearts (Mark 7:20-23). People will never find a solution to their problems until they agree with God's diagnosis of the cause—personal sin.

Romans 3:23—The passage around this verse informs us that there is no distinction among people: Both Jews and Gentiles have sinned and fallen short of God's standard of righteousness. Everyone is in the same situation.

Note: Occasionally, in order to focus attention on a particular thought, you will memorize a verse that is not a complete sentence. This is another reason why you should read the context of the verses as you begin to memorize them.

Isaiah 53:6 (Optional)—Isaiah stated that everyone has willfully turned his or her back on God, preferring to remain independent from God. This is part of the natural human condition (see Romans 3:10-12). Every person is infected and impacted by sin.

Your Weekly Plan

1. At the beginning of the week make sure you have your 3 x 5 verse cards for *Live the New Life* and *Beginning with Christ*—at least 11 verses.

2. Each day review all the verses you have memorized during Books 1 and 2.

3. Reread the steps on "How to Memorize a Verse Effectively" in the *Growing Strong in God's Family* workbook (pages 15-16).

4. A day or two before your next class session, write out your new verse from memory or quote it to someone to make sure you have learned it correctly.

How to Meditate on the Scriptures — Part 2

In session 1 you applied the first two techniques for meditating on the Scriptures: 1—paraphrase and 2—questions. In this session you experience four more approaches you can use for meditating on a Bible passage.

3—Prayer

Pray over the verse or passage. One way to do this is to think about each phrase or thought and pray about the implications for your life or for the lives of others. *The best things I prayed about while meditating on Romans 12:1 were:* _____

_____

_____

_____

_____

_____

_____

_____

4—Emphasis

Emphasize different words or phrases. Read or quote a verse aloud several times and stress a different word or phrase each time. This puts your focus on various facets. Each word adds its own significance to the passage. *The best thoughts I had while emphasizing different words in John 15:7 were:* _____

_____

_____

_____

_____

_____

_____

5—Cross-Reference

Find cross-references. Using a concordance or other Bible study aid, find additional verses which support the basic concept of the passage you are cross-referencing. *Other verses which say the same things as John 14:21 are:*

Reference _____ Thought _____

_____

_____

Reference _____ Thought _____

_____

_____

6—Application

Seek to make an application. Prayerfully reflect on the passage allowing God to show you how to apply its truths. Try to make your application a positive, specific step you will take. *In considering how Philippians 4:6-7 relates to my own circumstances, I had the following thoughts:* _____

_____

_____

_____

_____

_____

Introduction to Bible Study—Book 3

Having completed Books 1 and 2 in *The New 2:7 Series,* you have undoubtedly deepened your convictions about the profit of personal Bible study—what it means to search the Scriptures and discover truth. You have probably noticed that when you investigate the Word for yourself, it affects your attitudes and actions day by day.

However, even though you realize the importance of systematic Bible study, you will probably sense opposition as you continue. The enemy of every Christian, Satan himself, knows the power of God's Word, and he will try at every turn to keep you from it. You will find such excuses as, "You're too busy," or, "You can't concentrate now—do this little thing first, then get back to Bible study." You will find interruptions, temptations, and even criticism by others hindering you from giving your attention to Scripture.

Recognizing that Satan is the cause of such hindrances is helpful. It reemphasizes the importance of Bible study and can increase your determination to study. How do you win? Here are some practical suggestions:

1. Accept by faith the victory that Christ has already won over Satan and all his works. "Thanks be to God! He gives us the victory through our Lord Jesus Christ" (1 Corinthians 15:57).
2. Ask the Lord for wisdom and strength. "Call to me and I will answer you and tell you great and unsearchable things you do not know" (Jeremiah 33:3).
3. Use personal discipline. No spiritual exercise becomes automatic. Just as you must make an effort to keep up your daily quiet time with the Lord, so you must plan and zealously guard your study time. It is good to set a definite goal for a certain amount of study to be completed each week and to be diligent in reaching that goal. "A longing fulfilled is sweet to the soul," Solomon said (Proverbs 13:19), and reaching a planned objective brings satisfaction and further motivation.

4. Arrange with a friend to check you on your weekly goals in Bible study, and perhaps share something you have learned from it with him or her.

During Book 3 you will prepare and discuss Bible studies related to Christian character. Character has been defined as "moral excellence and firmness." God desires that we have strong, moral qualities in our inner lives as well as acceptable and effective outward behavior. Therefore, it is imperative that we learn what God's Word says about the character of the Christian. The five areas of Christian character you will study in this course are:

1. The Call to Fruitful Living
2. Love in Action
3. Purity of Life
4. Integrity in Living
5. Character in Action

ASSIGNMENT FOR SESSION 3:

1. Scripture Memory: Study and complete the "Scripture Memory Instructions—Week Three" (pages 25-26). Memorize the verse on "Sin's Penalty," Romans 6:23.
2. Quiet Time: Continue your Bible reading, marking, and recording.
3. Bible Study: Complete the Bible study, "The Call to Fruitful Living" (pages 26-33).
4. Evangelism: Come to class prepared to give your personal testimony with or without notes in less than four minutes.

SESSION 3

OUTLINE OF THIS SESSION:
1. Break into verse review groups and review the verse on "Sin's Penalty," Romans 6:23. (Work at getting anything signed that you can on your *Completion Record*.)
2. Share some quiet time thoughts from your *Bible Reading Highlights Record*.
3. Have two or three people give a personal testimony with or without notes in less than four minutes.
4. Discuss the Bible study, "The Call to Fruitful Living" (pages 26-33).
5. Read the "Assignment for Session 4" (page 33).
6. Have a short period of prayer for pre-Christians on your Evangelism Prayer List.

Scripture Memory Instructions — Week Three

About the Verses
TOPIC 2. SIN'S PENALTY

The fact that every person is a sinner has serious consequences.

Romans 6:23—Paul said that sin results in death. All will die physically some day, but all have already died spiritually. Spiritual death is separation from God. This is why even though most people believe in the existence of God, they have no personal fellowship with Him. They are separated from Him by an impassable gulf, which is the result of sin.

God is love, but He is also just. He cannot overlook sin and still remain both just or holy. The only thing a holy God can do to sin is judge it. The Bible says, "Whoever rejects the Son will not see life, for God's wrath remains on him [literally, 'hangs over his head']" (John 3:36). We may not like to think about it, but the Bible speaks as much of judgment as it does of almost any other topic. We need to know about it.

Hebrews 9:27 (Optional)—Every person has an appointment with death and judgment. The person without Christ cannot escape these imperatives. It is inevitable—every man and woman must give account of themselves to God.

Your Weekly Plan
1. At the beginning of the week make

sure you have your 3 x 5 verse cards for *Live the New Life* and *Beginning with Christ*.

2. Each day review all the verses you have memorized during Book 1 and Book 2 in *The New 2:7 Series*.

3. A day or two before your next class session, write out your new verse from memory or quote it to someone to make sure you have learned it correctly.

THE CALL TO FRUITFUL LIVING

Many people measure the fruitfulness of their lives by the quantity of their activities. This does not necessarily give a true picture of the quality of their lives. *What you are is more important than what you do.*

THINK ABOUT:
How do you think fruitfulness should be measured in the life of a Christian?

GOD'S DESIRE FOR YOUR FRUITFULNESS

1. Read John 15:5. Here Christ gives insight into the matter of spiritual fruit-bearing.

   a. In this analogy identify the vine and the branches. _____

   _____

   _____

   _____

   _____

   b. What condition is necessary for the branch to bear fruit? _____

   _____

   _____

   _____

   c. Why does the branch need the vine? _____

   _____

   _____

   _____

d. Explain what you think it means to "abide" or "remain" in Christ.

_____

_____

_____

2. What additional observations can you make about bearing fruit from John 15:8,16? _____

_____

_____

_____

_____

3. Read Galatians 5:22-23 and list the qualities God wants to produce in your life. Briefly define each one.

THE FRUIT OF THE SPIRIT	BRIEF DEFINITION OF THE FRUIT
1. _____	_____
2. _____	_____
3. _____	_____
4. _____	_____
5. _____	_____
6. _____	_____
7. _____	_____
8. _____	_____
9. _____	_____

Which of the qualities on page 27 is currently the most important to you and why?

_____

_____

_____

GROWING IN CHARACTER

4. Scripture reveals several important areas of life in which character is displayed. List one for each of the following verses.

Philippians 4:8 _____

Colossians 4:6 _____

1 Peter 2:12 _____

What is the relationship between these three areas? _____

_____

_____

_____

5. Carefully examine 2 Peter 1:1-8. This portion of Scripture deals with the subject of growth in Christian character.
   a. How has God equipped you to grow in character? Verses 2-4 _____

   _____

   _____

   _____

   b. What does verse 8 say about fruitfulness? _____

   _____

   _____

   _____

   c. List eight aspects of Christian character.

   _____   _____

   _____   _____

   _____   _____

   _____   _____

How might their sequence be significant?

_____

_____

_____

d. Choose three of these qualities and write a definition for each which adequately expresses what you understand the quality to mean.

   1. _____

      _____

   2. _____

      _____

   3. _____

e. Select one quality which you would like to strengthen. With God's help, what steps could you take to become more Christlike in displaying that quality? _____

_____

_____

_____

_____

> *Sow a thought, reap an act;*
> *Sow an act, reap a habit;*
> *Sow a habit, reap a character;*
> *Sow a character, reap a destiny.*

GROWING IN WISDOM

6. One of the purposes of the Book of Proverbs is that people might attain wisdom. What do the following verses teach about wisdom?

Proverbs 2:6 _____

Proverbs 3:13-14 _____

Proverbs 9:10 _____

Proverbs 11:2 _____

Proverbs 24:13-14 _____

7. Read James 3:13-18

   a. How is godly wisdom displayed? _____

   _____

   _____

   b. List the characteristics of godly wisdom and ungodly wisdom. Verses 15-17

GODLY WISDOM	UNGODLY WISDOM

   c. Which of the preceding characteristics have influenced our society the most? Explain your answer. _____

   _____

   _____

   _____

   _____

   _____

   _____

   _____

*Wisdom is more than knowledge, which is the accumulation of facts . . .
it is the right application of knowledge in moral and spiritual matters.*

—J. Oswald Sanders

CHANGING ATTITUDES

   8. Read Philippians 3:4-14.

   a. List several of Paul's new attitudes and patterns which differed from his former ones.

PAUL'S FORMER ATTITUDES AND PATTERNS (VERSES 4-7)	PAUL'S NEW ATTITUDES AND PATTERNS (VERSES 7-14)
1. Put confidence in the flesh	_____
2. Religious leader	_____
3. Persecuted the church	_____
4. Blameless in the law	_____
5. Counted all as gain for self	_____

   b. Why do you feel Paul had such a positive attitude about the future?

   _____

   _____

   _____

   _____

   _____

   _____

   _____

   9. In the Sermon on the Mount, Jesus Christ gives eight basic ingredients for living a holy, happy life. From Matthew 5:3-12, list the blessing that He promises to the person with each quality.

KIND OF PERSON	JESUS' PROMISE
a. The poor in spirit (recognizing one's own poverty in spiritual things). Verse 3	_____
b. Person who mourns (is genuinely sorry for sin). Verse 4	_____
c. The meek (having strength under control). Verse 5	_____
d. Person who hungers for righteousness (deep concern for holiness). Verse 6	_____

e. The merciful (compassionate).
Verse 7   _____

f. The pure in heart (free from moral
sin). Verse 8   _____

g. The peacemaker (promotes peace
by reconciling others). Verse 9   _____

h. The one persecuted (oppressed for
Christ's sake). Verses 10-11   _____

10. In which one of the above areas are you currently the strongest?

_____

_____

In which one are you the weakest? _____

_____

SUMMARY
Review the chapter subtopics and write your own summary of each section.

God's Desire for Your Fruitfulness

_____

_____

_____

_____

_____

Growing in Character

_____

_____

_____

_____

Growing in Wisdom

_____

_____

_____

_____

_____

Changing Attitudes

_____

_____

_____

_____

_____

ASSIGNMENT FOR SESSION 4:
   1. Scripture Memory: Study and complete the "Scripture Memory
      Instructions—Week Four" (page 34). Memorize the verse on "Christ
      Paid the Penalty," Romans 5:8.
   2. Quiet Time: Continue your Bible reading, marking, and recording.
   3. Bible Study: Complete the "Relationship Evangelism Bible Study" (pages 35-
      38).
   4. Evangelism: Come to class prepared to give your personal testimony with or
      without notes in less than four minutes.

SESSION 4

OUTLINE OF THIS SESSION:

1. Break into verse review groups and quote the verse on "Christ Paid the Penalty," Romans 5:8. (Work at getting anything signed that you can on your *Completion Record*.)
2. Share some quiet time thoughts from your *Bible Reading Highlights Record*.
3. Have two or three people give a personal testimony with or without notes in less than four minutes.
4. Discuss the "Relationship Evangelism Bible Study" (pages 35-38).
5. Read the "Assignment for Session 5" (page 38).
6. Close in prayer.

Scripture Memory Instructions — Week Four

About the Verses

TOPIC 3. CHRIST PAID THE PENALTY

Either we must suffer the punishment for our sins and be separated from God throughout eternity, or someone else must pay the penalty so we can go free. Only Jesus Christ, the sinless, perfect God-man, could do this for us.

Romans 5:8 — Paul said that God showed His great love for us by sending Christ to die in our place, even while we were still undeserving sinners. This is pure love and grace.

1 Peter 3:18 (Optional) — Peter told why Christ, the Righteous One, died for us — the unrighteous ones. He did it "to bring us to God" — to bridge the gulf that separated us from God's presence and a personal relationship with Him.

On the cross God placed our sins on His Son. Jesus Christ bore our penalty, which is separation from the Father. That is why Jesus cried, "My God, my God, why have you forsaken me?" (Matthew 27:46). The Father had to turn away from His Son because in that moment He was made sin for us. Now, instead of our sins, we have Christ's righteousness imparted to us, and we can enter the very presence of God.

Your Weekly Plan

1. Remember, always say the topic first, then the reference, the verse, and the reference again at the end.

2. Each day review all the verses you have memorized during Book 1 and Book 2 in *The New 2:7 Series*.

3. By the end of the week check your new verse by writing it out from memory or quoting it to someone else.

RELATIONSHIP EVANGELISM BIBLE STUDY

TWO KEY INGREDIENTS

The Scriptures give us insight into how the gospel can have its greatest impact. There are two key ingredients: preaching (or proclaiming) the gospel, and affirming (or modeling) the gospel message through the life of a believer. This study will help you understand the scriptural basis for proclaiming and modeling the message.

PROCLAIMING THE GOSPEL

1. According to 2 Corinthians 5:18-20, with what have we been entrusted, as Christians? _____

   _____

   _____

2. What are Christians commanded to do in Mark 16:15? _____

   _____

   _____

3. What does Paul see as his life purpose in Ephesians 3:7-8? _____

   _____

   _____

4. Write a brief summary of the Christian's responsibility in proclaiming the gospel from the above verses. _____

   _____

   _____

   _____

In addition to proclaiming the gospel, the Christian is directed to affirm or display the reality of the Christian message in his or her own life. In this way the pre-Christian not only hears but sees what it means to come into a relationship with Jesus Christ.

AFFIRMING THE GOSPEL

5. How does Christ instruct us to relate to the pre-Christians around us? Matthew 5:13-16 _____

   _____

   _____

6. In Philippians 2:14-15 how do our lives function in affirming the gospel?

_____

_____

_____

7. From the following verses list some of the ways we are to relate to non-Christians: Matthew 5:43-48; Luke 14:12-14; Colossians 4:5-6; 2 Corinthians 4:5. _____

_____

_____

_____

_____

_____

How do the above actions and attitudes affirm the gospel? _____

_____

_____

_____

_____

_____

8. From Matthew 9:10-13, explain how Jesus Christ related to unbelievers and what His purpose was. _____

_____

_____

9. Why is a relationship with a person necessary to affirm the gospel?

_____

_____

_____

THE PROCESS OF RELATIONSHIP EVANGELISM

"My food," said Jesus, "is to do the will of him who sent me and to finish his work. Do you not say, 'Four months more and then the harvest'? I tell you, open your eyes and look at the fields! They are ripe for harvest. Even now

the reaper draws his wages, even now he harvests the crop for eternal life,
so that the sower and the reaper may be glad together. Thus the saying 'One
sows and another reaps' is true. I sent you to reap what you have not
worked for. Others have done the hard work, and you have reaped the bene-
fits of their labor."

—John 4:34-38

In John 4:34-38, seeing people come to Christ is equated with reaping a harvest; it is the final step in a series of activities. A harvest must be preceded by breaking up ground, sowing, watering, growing, and finally, reaping. Christ tells us that when we are involved in reaping (seeing someone come to Christ), much preliminary labor has already been done by others.

10. Before coming to Christ what are some literal ways that planting, watering, and growing might take place in a nonChristian's life? John 4:34-38

_____

_____

_____

_____

_____

11. In 1 Corinthians 3:5-9 Paul describes a real example of how planting, watering, and growing took place.
   a. What does verse 8 say about the importance of sowing and reaping?

_____

_____

_____

   b. Who is responsible for growth? Verse 7 _____

_____

_____

   c. What is the individual Christian's responsibility? Verses 5, 8, 9

_____

_____

SUMMARY

The Christian has been provided with two primary means to win the world to Christ: the message of the gospel and the reality of the gospel in the Christian's life. These two means are effective in reaching both the religious and the secular person. Relationship Evangelism is primarily the process of adapting the two means to the best advantage of the person we are seeking to lead to Christ. Relationship Evangelism is a process, and its length will be determined to a great extent by how much or how little labor has been done before we enter into the picture with the individual. Nevertheless, the ultimate results of evangelism are dependent upon God who "gives the growth" and the individual who must, through an act of his will, voluntarily receive Christ as Savior and Lord.

ASSIGNMENT FOR SESSION 5:

1. Scripture Memory: Study and complete the "Scripture Memory Instructions—Week Five" (page 39). Memorize the verse on "Salvation Not by Works," Ephesians 2:8-9.
2. Quiet Time: Continue your Bible reading, marking, and recording.
3. Bible Study: Complete the Bible study, "Love in Action" (pages 40-45).
4. Evangelism: Come to class prepared to give your personal testimony with or without notes in less than four minutes.

SESSION 5

OUTLINE OF THIS SESSION:
1. Break into verse review groups and quote the verse on "Salvation Not by Works," Ephesians 2:8-9. (Work at getting anything signed that you can on your *Completion Record.*)
2. Share some quiet time thoughts from your *Bible Reading Highlights Record.*
3. Have two or three people give a personal testimony with or without notes in less than four minutes.
4. Discuss the Bible study, "Love in Action" (pages 40-45).
5. Read the "Assignment for Session 6" (page 45).
6. Close in prayer.

Scripture Memory Instructions — Week Five

About the Verses
TOPIC 4. SALVATION NOT BY WORKS

Many people have the idea that their eternal destiny will be decided by their good deeds being weighed against their bad ones. So, they try to earn or solicit God's mercy by good and charitable acts that will blind God to their shortcomings and moral failures.

Ephesians 2:8-9—Paul made it clear that salvation is not by our works, but only by God's grace. Through Christ we receive unearned and unmerited favor. Salvation is a gift we receive by faith. If we could work for salvation, we could then boast that we had attained it. But God alone must receive the credit for saving us.

Titus 3:5 (Optional)—Here again Paul stated that we are not saved by our own efforts, but by God's merciful action. This is hard for some people to accept. It goes against a person's independent nature and "do-it-yourself" philosophy of life. To be saved means we are cleansed of our sins and spiritually born anew. This is a work of the Holy Spirit, who causes regeneration in us. He washes us clean.

Your Weekly Plan
1. Read the context of your new verse in your Bible to help you understand its setting.

2. Each day review all the verses you have memorized. Use your 3 x 5 cards for review as well as for memorization.

3. Strive for word perfection, and check your new verse by the end of the week by writing it out or quoting it to someone else.

LOVE IN ACTION

Today people have many different definitions of love. Most of these come from the illustrations of love found in movies, on television, in advertisements and magazines, and, perhaps, from personal experience. The Scriptures speak directly about love. The Bible tells us what love is, and how we may demonstrate it.

> **THINK ABOUT IT:** Generally what is the world's concept of love?

WHAT IS GENUINE LOVE?

1. How is love defined?

a. Using a secular dictionary, define love. _____

_____

_____

_____

b. Using a Bible dictionary, define love. _____

_____

_____

_____

c. How do the two differ? _____

_____

_____

_____

2. First Corinthians 13:4-8 gives some of the characteristics of Biblical love.

a. Fill in the chart below.

WHAT LOVE IS	WHAT LOVE IS NOT

b. What are two or three major conclusions you can make about love based on this passage? _____

_____

_____

_____

_____

3. Carefully read 1 John 4:8-21.
   a. What important fact about God do you see in verses 8 and 16?

   _____

   _____

   b. What has God done to demonstrate His love for us? _____

   _____

   _____

   c. Because of God's love for us, what should our response be? Verses 11, 19

   _____

   _____

   d. To what degree can love and fear exist together? Verse 18 _____

   _____

   _____

THE FOCUS OF YOUR LOVE

4. From the passages you have studied, define love in your own words.

   _____

   _____

   _____

5. Read John 13:34-35.
   a. What is one of the surest evidences that you are a follower of Christ?

   _____

   _____

   b. Why do you think Jesus placed such emphasis on demonstrating love?

   _____

   _____

Love enters into our everyday actions in a variety of ways. Many people relate to others with only the tacit agreement: "If you do your part, I'll do mine." This conditional way of giving of ourselves is not love. God wants us to say, "I'll love you even if I receive nothing in return." It is this selfless giving and loving which God develops in our attitudes and actions.

LOVE IN HUMILITY

6. Humility comes from having the right perspective about God and yourself. What do the following verses tell you about your perspective toward God and toward yourself?

Jeremiah 9:23-24 _____

Philippians 2:3 _____

7. Read 1 Peter 5:5-6.
   a. What does the passage teach about humility? _____

   _____

   _____

   b. Why do you think God places such a high value on humility in a person's life? _____

   _____

   _____

8. Consider Romans 12:3.
   a. What error must you be careful to avoid? _____

   _____

   _____

   b. What are the results of overestimating yourself? _____

   _____

   _____

   c. What are the results of underestimating yourself? _____

   _____

   _____

   Both situations in this illustration are manifestations of pride because the person is preoccupied with self.

PRIDE

Thinking too highly of self: "God's work can't get along without me!"	Thinking too lowly of self: "God can't do anything through me!"

9. Summarize the relationship between love and humility. _____

_____

_____

_____

LOVE IN SPEECH AND ACTION

10. Read Colossians 4:6 and write a paraphrase of the verse. _____

_____

_____

_____

_____

11. God can give you gracious and loving words. What can the right words do?

Proverbs 12:25 _____

Proverbs 15:23 _____

Proverbs 16:24 _____

Proverbs 23:16 _____

Love is not merely an inner feeling, but also an act of the will. Love can be known only by the action it produces.

12. Read 1 John 3:16-18. Indicate how love can be demonstrated toward others.

_____

_____

_____

13. List some practical ways that you personally can demonstrate love toward Christians and nonChristians.

Christians

_____

_____

_____

_____

NonChristians

_____

_____

_____

_____

> *To love the whole world*
> *For me is no chore;*
> *My only real problem's*
> *My neighbor next door.*

SUMMARY

Review the chapter subtopics and write your own summary of each section.

What Is Genuine Love?

_____

_____

_____

_____

_____

_____

The Focus of Your Love

_____

_____

_____

_____

Love in Humility

_____

_____

_____

_____

_____

Love in Speech and Action

_____

_____

_____

_____

_____

ASSIGNMENT FOR SESSION 6:
1. Scripture Memory: Study and complete the "Scripture Memory Instructions—Week Six" (pages 46-47). Memorize the verse on "Must Receive Christ," John 1:12.
2. Quiet Time: Continue your Bible reading, marking, and recording.
3. Bible Study: Complete the Bible study, "Purity of Life" (pages 47-53).

SESSION 6

OUTLINE OF THIS SESSION:
1. Break into verse review groups and quote the verse on "Must Receive Christ," John 1:12.
2. Share some quiet time thoughts from your *Bible Reading Highlights Record*.
3. Discuss the Bible study, "Purity of Life" (pages 47-53).
4. Read the "Assignment for Session 7" (page 53).
5. Close in prayer.

Scripture Memory Instructions — Week Six

About the Verses

TOPIC 5. MUST RECEIVE CHRIST

The New Testament teaches that we are saved solely by believing in Jesus Christ. Nothing else is required. Today, *believe* often means merely to give mental assent. Many say, "Oh yes, I believe in God." But in the Bible, belief means completely trusting and resolutely committing oneself to Jesus Christ as Savior from sin. Paul wrote, "For in the gospel a righteousness from God is revealed, a righteousness that is by faith from first to last, just as it is written: 'The righteous will live by faith'" (Romans 1:17). Faith in what the Bible says requires a positive action; believing means doing something. In your memory verse for this week, the importance of both believing and verbalizing that belief is stressed.

John 1:12—John equated receiving Jesus Christ with believing in Him.

This is how one becomes a child of God. Everyone is familiar with the act of receiving a gift. One simply takes it and thanks the person who gave it, and then enjoys the gift.

Romans 10:9-10 (Optional)—There is a point in time when a person comes to know and believe the gospel. He or she understands the substitutionary death of Christ on the cross, the forgiveness of sin, and Christ's rightful ownership over one's life. They realize in their heart and mind "I now understand what Christ did on the cross and I know He died for me."

It is important for this person to confirm his or her faith in Christ by verbally acknowledging Christ as Savior and Lord. A practical way to do this is to (1) thank God in prayer for forgiveness and eternal life through Christ and (2) to state clearly to another individual that he or she has believed in and accepted Christ's gospel.

Your Weekly Plan

1. By now you have learned the importance of starting promptly each week to begin learning a new verse the very first day after your class.

2. Learn your new verse and review your old ones as you have been doing the last few weeks.

3. At the end of the week check your new verse by writing it out or quoting it to someone else.

PURITY OF LIFE

It has been stated, "The new morality is nothing more than the old immorality in modern clothes." As society experiences moral decline, it becomes less popular for the Christian to take a stand on the moral absolutes of God's Word. Though freedom from all moral responsibility is sought by many people, Christians will only find God's greatest blessing by continuing to live by God's Word.

THINK ABOUT:
Generally what does the world use as standards for evaluating morality?

GOD'S STANDARD

1. What is God's standard for purity? 1 Peter 1:15-16 _____

_____

_____

_____

How do you think God expects us to live up to this standard? _____

_____

_____

_____

_____

2. What are some ways we are to demonstrate God's standard?

Matthew 5:21-22 _____

_____

Matthew 5:27-28 _____

_____

Romans 12:1-2 _____

_____

2 Corinthians 7:1 _____

_____

Every man has a train of thought on which he rides when he is alone. The dignity and nobility of his life, as well as his happiness, depend upon the direction in which that train is going, the baggage it carries and the scenery through which it travels.

—Joseph Fort Newton

3. Study Colossians 1:21-23.

   a. What has God done to insure our holiness? _____

   _____

   _____

   b. What must we do? _____

   _____

   _____

THE IMPORTANCE OF PERSONAL PURITY

4. Read 1 Corinthians 6:12-20.

   a. List several reasons why we should avoid immorality. _____

   _____

   _____

   _____

   _____

   b. How do you think immoral behavior affects our relationship with God?

   _____

   _____

   _____

c. How does it affect our relationship with others? (Consider both Christians and nonChristians.) _____

_____

_____

_____

_____

_____

5. The world's standards differ greatly from God's. From 1 John 2:15-16, what are some characteristics of men and women that reflect the world's standards? List and define these on the chart below.

CHARACTERISTIC	DEFINITION

6. What do the Scriptures say to the following excuses for wrong moral behavior?

a. "Since everyone else does it, it must be right."

Proverbs 14:12 _____

_____

b. "I only need to discover what is right for me."

Ecclesiastes 11:9 _____

_____

c. "Nobody will ever find out that I did it."

Hebrews 4:13 _____

_____

d. "I'll stop after this one time."

Galatians 6:7-8 _____

_____

   e. "I didn't really *do* anything—all I did was *think* it."

     Matthew 5:28 _____

     _____

7. The battle for purity is fought in the mind. Read Romans 8:5-8.

   a. What two types of people are referred to in the passage? _____

     _____

     _____

   b. What are the results of each mindset? _____

     _____

     _____

     _____

8. On what should we choose to focus our thoughts? Philippians 4:8

     _____

     _____

   Suggest some practical ways in which to motivate yourself to dwell on these
   things. _____

     _____

     _____

     _____

     _____

     _____

Try to forget the number 13. When you have forgotten it, check this box: ☐
This is how some people try to avoid immorality—they think they can just make
themselves not think about it. It is impossible to eliminate a wrong thought from
your mind unless you substitute something good in its place. How might
Scripture memory and meditation improve your thought life? _____

_____

_____

_____

_____

THE PATH TO PURITY

9. Read Ephesians 4:17-24.

a. How does the passage describe the nonChristian's walk? _____

_____

_____

_____

_____

b. What steps should Christians take to overcome their former way of life?
Verses 22-24 _____

_____

_____

_____

_____

c. What are some practical ways to do this? _____

_____

_____

_____

_____

10. What can we do to live a clean life, pleasing to the Lord?

Psalm 119:9-11 _____

_____

Proverbs 4:14-15_____

_____

Romans 13:14 _____

_____

Galatians 5:16_____

_____

11. Study Genesis 39:7-12 and 2 Samuel 11:1-4. Compare the events in
Joseph's and David's lives.

	JOSEPH	DAVID
a. What were the surrounding circumstances?		
b. What were their respective attitudes?		
c. What were their resulting actions?		

d. Why do you think these two men responded in different ways to a similar situation? _____

_____

_____

_____

12. What scriptural standards do you have concerning your relationship with the opposite sex? State two of them. _____

_____

_____

_____

Food was meant for the stomach and the stomach for food; but God has no permanent purpose for either. But you cannot say that our physical body was made for sexual promiscuity; it was made for God, and God is the answer to our deepest longings.

—1 Corinthians 6:13 (PH)

SUMMARY
Review the chapter subtopics and write your own summary of each section.

God's Standard

_____

_____

_____

_____

_____

_____

The Importance of Personal Purity

_____

_____

_____

_____

_____

_____

The Path to Purity

_____

_____

_____

_____

_____

_____

ASSIGNMENT FOR SESSION 7:
1. Scripture Memory: Study and complete the "Scripture Memory Instructions—Week Seven" (pages 54-55). Memorize the verse on "Assurance of Salvation," 1 John 5:13.
2. Quiet Time: Continue your Bible reading, marking, and recording.
3. Evangelism:
   a. Come to class prepared to give your personal testimony with or without notes in less than four minutes.
   b. Read the material on *The Bridge Illustration* (pages 55-64) and be prepared to discuss it in class.

SESSION 7

OUTLINE OF THIS SESSION:
1. Break into verse review groups and quote the verse on "Assurance of Salvation," 1 John 5:13.
2. Share some quiet time thoughts from your *Bible Reading Highlights Record.*
3. Have two or three people give a personal testimony with or without notes in less than four minutes.
4. Discuss *The Bridge Illustration* (pages 55-64).
5. Read the "Assignment for Session 8" (page 65).
6. Close in prayer.

Scripture Memory Instructions — Week Seven

About the Verses
TOPIC 6. ASSURANCE OF SALVATION

It is nearly impossible to build a solid structure on a shaky foundation. And it is very difficult to grow in the Christian life properly if one is unsure of his or her salvation. Some Christians do not believe they can know they have eternal life. Others gauge the assurance of their salvation by their feelings, a most unstable foundation. But God wants us to *know* we have eternal life.

1 John 5:13—John stated clearly that his primary objective in this epistle was to help those who believe in Jesus Christ to know that they have eternal life.

But how can we know? One evidence is our desire to please God, resulting from the Holy Spirit's residence in our bodies. Other evidences of new life in Christ are the desires to read His Word, to commune with Him in prayer, to fellowship with other believers, and to tell others about Christ. But the foundation on which all evidence rests is the promise of God's Word.

John 5:24 (Optional)—Jesus said if we hear His Word and believe on the Father through Christ, we have eternal life. This eternal life is a *present* possession. We will never have to face judgment for our sins because the moment we believe, we pass from spiritual death to spiritual life. The primary basis for assurance of salvation is to believe what God says about it—what He has promised.

Your Weekly Plan
1. During your daily review time give special attention to your newest memory verses. Don't rush through the review.

Think about the meaning and implications of the verses for your own life.

2. Use spare moments during the day for memorizing and for review. You should have no difficulty in reviewing daily all the verses you have memorized in *The New 2:7 Series*.

3. At the end of the week check your new verse by writing it out or quoting it to someone else.

The Bridge Illustration
How to Use "The Bridge" to Communicate the Gospel

The Bridge Illustration is one of many effective methods for presenting the gospel. It has been used successfully to communicate the gospel over many years and in many contexts, in groups and person-to-person. You will find it to be a useful and powerful tool to aid you in explaining the gospel.

Many variations of *The Bridge Illustration* are in use. The presentation described here is relatively simple and straightforward. Your group leader may ask you to make adjustments to the format presented here in your workbook. Learn the method he or she presents, and become skilled in that method. After you have used this method to present the gospel to several people, you may want to make a few adjustments in the format to make it more your own. This illustration will become a sharpened tool in your hands if these adjustments are based on experience in communicating the gospel to actual people.

FLEXIBILITY
The Bridge Illustration can take as little as 10 minutes to present, or it can be stretched out to an hour or more. A normal presentation will last 15 to 30 minutes. The flexibility of this presentation is one of its greatest assets. It can be tailored specifically to a person or situation.

SENSITIVITY
The way in which the Holy Spirit leads you to witness will vary in different situations. It is important to be observant and sensitive as you are relating to the person with whom you are sharing The Bridge. In any type of ministry situation it is important to pray silently and to ask God for guidance and wisdom, and for the ability to communicate the gospel clearly.

THE LEAD-IN
Experience has shown that it is helpful to have a few statements and questions in mind to help open the door for presenting the gospel. Often an ideal time to share the gospel is after a person has heard a testimony—yours or someone else's. You first want to get that person's response to the testimony he or she has heard by saying something like:

"Well, that's my story. What do you think?"

Or, "Well, you just heard her story. What is your reaction to what happened to her?" A more direct lead-in is: "How about you, Pat? Have you ever thought much about becoming a Christian?"

If there is time to talk further and the person still shows interest and a capacity to hear more, you might say something like, "You know, Jim, there's a diagram that summarizes and clarifies what it means to become a real Christian and to know with certainty that you have eternal life. If you have a few more minutes, may I sketch it out for you?" When he says, "Yes," you may proceed.

If you feel the person has heard as much as he or she can absorb at the time, you might say something like: "You know, Pat, there is a diagram that clarifies what it means to be a real Christian and to know for certain that you have eternal life. When you have 15 or 20 minutes sometime, why don't we sit down and I will sketch it out for you? OK?" Then, at a later, appropriate time, you ask permission and go through the illustration.

In many situations you will find it natural to ask permission to draw out the illustration without having given your testimony.

PRESENTATION

One of the most effective ways to present the gospel using *The Bridge Illustration* is to ask questions about Scriptures which will enable a person to see each truth directly from God's Word. You will need to convey four concepts as you draw out The Bridge:

> 1. **God's Purpose**— *Abundant Life,* John 10:10
> *Eternal Life,* John 3:16
> 2. **Our Problem**— *All Have Sinned,* Ro. 3:23; Isaiah 53:6
> *Sin's Penalty,* Ro. 6:23; Heb. 9:27
> 3. **God's Remedy**— *Christ Paid the Penalty,* Ro. 5:8; 1 Peter 3:18
> *Salvation Not by Works,* Eph. 2:8-9; Titus 3:5
> 4. **Our Response**— *Must Receive Christ,* John 1:12; Ro. 10:9-10
> *Assurance of Salvation,* John 5:24; 1 John 5:13

The diagrams on pages 57-60 show how your illustration will develop as you present it. The printed text shows how you can use questions to present this material. You should note that each segment is introduced by a transition statement, followed by one or more questions. After the person has had a chance to state his or her observations, you should clarify and summarize each point and then make the transition to the next passage.

GOD'S PURPOSE

Let's look at two Bible verses that tell about some of the things God wants for us.

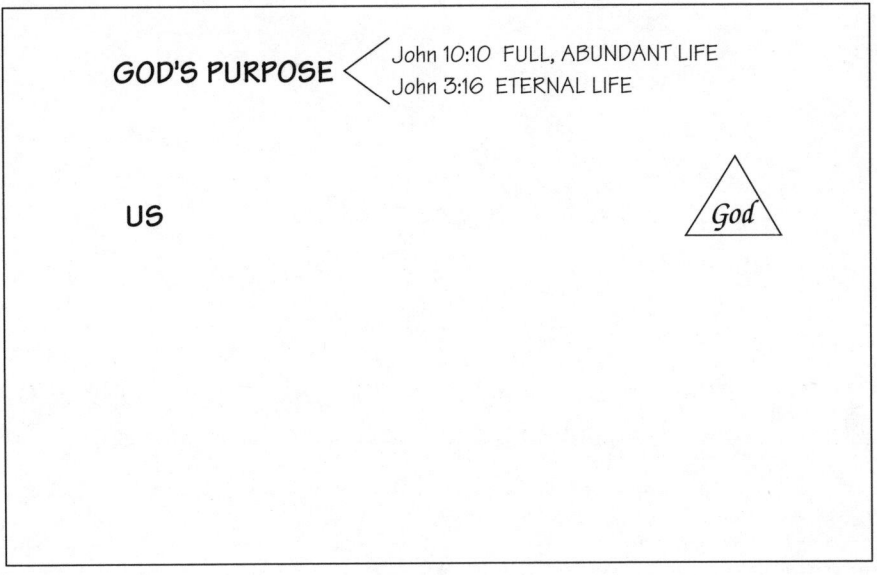

GOD'S PURPOSE — John 10:10 FULL, ABUNDANT LIFE / John 3:16 ETERNAL LIFE

US   God

John 10:10
Question: What does this passage say is one of God's reasons for sending His son?

Transition: God wants us to experience a full, abundant life. This would include such things as love, peace, purpose, and fulfillment.

John 3:16
Question: What additional reason do you see for God sending His son?

Transition: So, then, from these statements we can say that God wants us to experience a full, abundant life now and eternal life both in this life and after death.

OUR PROBLEM

But we have a problem. God did not create us like a robot who would automatically love and have fellowship with Him in return. He gave us a will and the freedom of choice. Let's look at what people are like—apart from God.

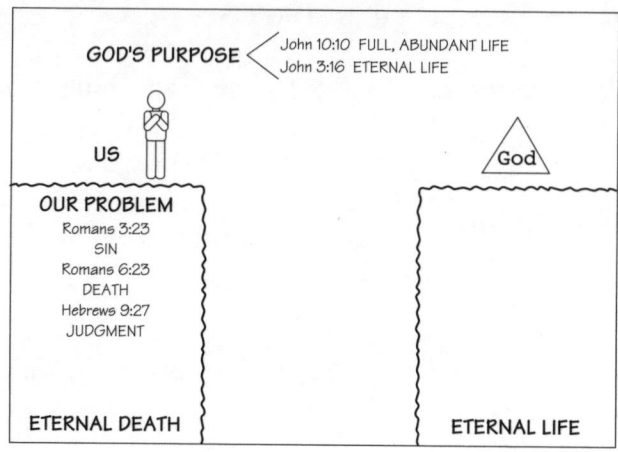

Romans 3:23

Question: What does this verse say about all people? Does this include me? Does this include you? How would you describe sin according to this verse?

Transition: Have you ever wondered what effect our sin has? Let's look at some other passages.

Romans 6:23

Question: How would you define wages? What do we earn? How would you describe death?

Transition: Let's look at another result of sin.

Hebrews 9:27

Question: What is one thing death brings with it?

Comment: You can see by this statement that each of us will die physically, and after we die physically we will face judgment.

Transition: So we can see that when we look at the condition of a person apart from God, it isn't very encouraging. We have sinned, and the penalty of sin is eternal death (separation from God). Also we see that the consequences of our sin bring about the judgment of God. Sin separates us from God.

GOD'S REMEDY

In spite of the fact that we have turned our backs on God and have disobeyed Him, He has provided a remedy so that we can know Him personally. He wants to give us both full, abundant life and eternal life. Only one bridge can cross the gulf that exists between a person and God, and that bridge is Jesus Christ, through His death on the cross.

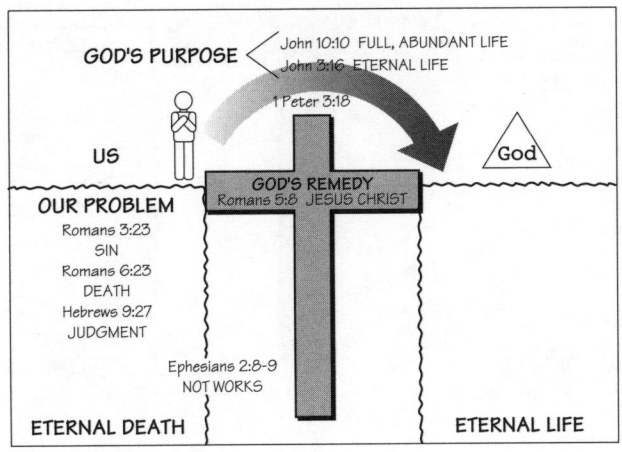

Romans 5:8

Question: Did God want us to become worthy before He provided a solution? What did God's love cause Him to do? _____

_____

People use many approaches in trying to find favor with God and to secure eternal life.

Ephesians 2:8-9

Question: What does the Bible say about the relationship between salvation and our efforts to be good? What is one reason God won't accept our good deeds as payment for our sins? _____

Transition: Let's look at another passage that explains this further.

1 Peter 3:18 (You should explain this passage phrase by phrase so that the gospel is clearly covered. This is an excellent verse to emphasize the good news of Christ's resurrection.)

OUR RESPONSE

Real belief results in a response on our part. Christ has made it possible for us to cross over to God's side and experience the full life He wants us to have. But we are not automatically on God's side.

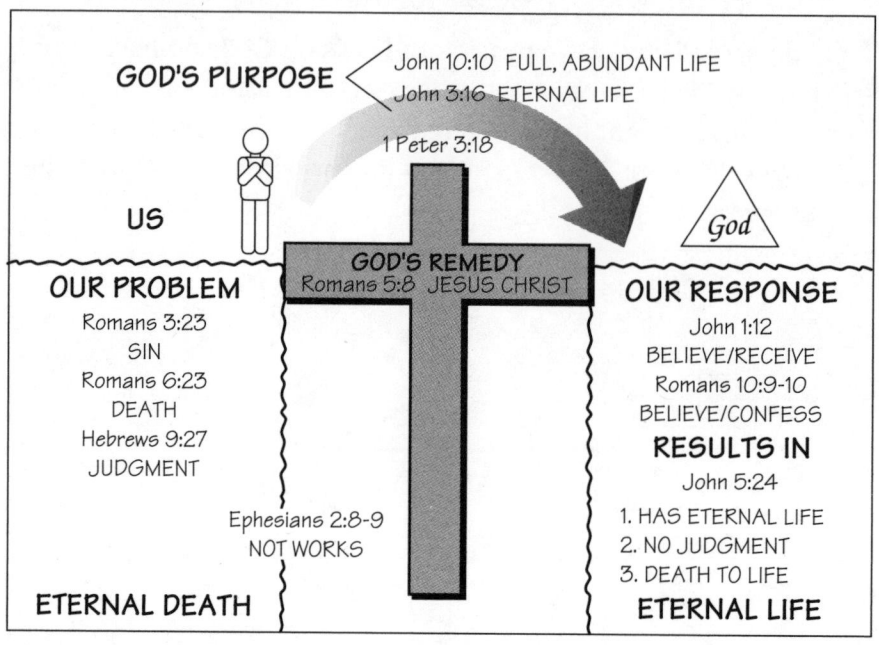

John 1:12
Question: What does this passage equate with believing? What does receiving Christ mean to you? (At this point, clarify that believing and receiving involve our mind, our emotions, and our will.)

Transition: A verse which can be used to illustrate how people might express their faith and belief that Jesus is their Savior is Romans 10:9-10.

Romans 10:9-10
Question: What two things does this passage say are necessary for salvation? If you respond in this way, of what can you be assured?

Transition: Let me summarize all of this with one important verse — John 5:24.

John 5:24
Question: What two things must we do according to this statement? What three results does Jesus promise to those who believe in Him?

Comment: God does not want us to wonder if we have eternal life. He wants us to be certain. The Bible says, "I write these things to you who believe in the name of the Son of God so that you may know that you have eternal life" (1 John 5:13).

PERSONAL INVITATION

Assume that you have been sharing the gospel with Susan. You might use the following suggestions to help her move toward a personal commitment.

1. "Does this make sense to you?"
2. "Do you have any questions about it?"
3. "Where would you place yourself in this illustration?"
   a. If Susan says, "On God's side," you might ask when she received Christ. Ask her to relate the specifics of her experience in receiving Christ.
   b. If she points to the left side or to the chasm, inquire, "What would you have to believe to be on God's side?" See if she can clearly communicate the issues of the gospel and the necessity of believing in Christ. You might say, "Is there any reason why you shouldn't cross over to God's side and be certain of eternal life?"
4. If she indicates a responsiveness to the gospel, ask, "Would you like to trust in (receive) Jesus Christ now? If so, I would be happy to pray with you."
5. If you believe she understands the gospel but is not yet ready to commit her life to Christ, encourage her to give these things further thought and consideration. Be sure, in a few days, to talk with her about the gospel and/or get her involved in some type of an investigative Bible study.
6. Whatever response she has, be sure she understands what she would specifically pray to affirm her faith in Christ. It is as simple as A-B-C:

   A—Acknowledge your sin and be willing to turn from it

   B—Believe Christ died for your sins and rose again

   C—Commit your life to Christ as Savior and Lord

   Note that these 3 points correspond to:

   A—Our Problem

   B—God's Remedy

   C—Our Response

PRACTICAL SUGGESTIONS

1. Do not memorize *The Bridge Illustration*. Learn the principles, ideas, verses, and key sentences. Make it your own.
2. Make an outline of the presentation as you would like to give it, and practice giving it by yourself.
3. Draw the illustration as you talk. This is an attention-getter.
4. Use a Bible rather than quoting verses. Have the nonChristian read them out of the Bible.
5. If the nonChristian brings up objections during your presentation, you

might say, "That's a good question. For the sake of continuity, may I try to answer that after completing the illustration?"

6. The ultimate goal is to bring a person to salvation in Christ. Proceed as far as the Holy Spirit gives you freedom. If the nonChristian is open to receive Christ, then have him or her pray.

YOUR PRESENTATIONS

In this course as you present The Bridge, you are not expected to use all of the interactive questions that are provided for you. First, you draw out The Bridge outline. This means the visual things—the words, the cliffs, the cross, and the Bible references. Then, twice during the course you will draw out The Bridge while you verbally explain it. Plan to communicate The Bridge a little more clearly each time. Practice alone before you make each of your presentations.

SAMPLE: HOW YOUR TWO PRESENTATIONS MIGHT SOUND

It is not required, but if you have time you are welcome to learn some of the questions and transitional statements suggested in this chapter. After this course you may want to set aside time to learn the questions and transitional statements.

Here is a sample of what your "lecture" type of presentation might sound like when you give it to one of your classmates. (Ask your classmate to read each of the verses aloud, but he or she should not ask questions or interact with you. For a change of pace you may read a verse here and there.)

As you think of the meaning of each verse and learn the sequence for drawing The Bridge, you will probably make a better presentation than this following brief sample.

> "First let's look at a couple verses that explain what **God's Purpose** is for you and me. Let's look at the book of John, chapter 10 and verse 10. [The verse is read aloud.] As you can see, it says that God wants us to have a full, abundant, quality kind of life. He really wants the best for us. Let's read John 3:16. [The verse is read aloud.] So, you see in John 3:16 that God also wants us to have eternal life so we can live with Him after this life.
>
> "But, we must look next at **Our Problem**. Why are all people not experiencing the full life God wants for us? We need to look at Romans 3:23. [The verse is read aloud.] We see that I have sinned and you have sinned. Every person in the world has done things

morally wrong in God's eyes — to various degrees. Let's read Romans 6:23. [The verse is read aloud.] We see in Romans 6:23 that the penalty for our sin is eternal death. We need forgiveness for our sins. Now let's read Hebrews 9:27. [The verse is read aloud.] So, Hebrews 9:27 tells us that if we don't receive forgiveness for our sins at some point in this life, after we die God will be our judge and He will reluctantly assign to us a severe penalty for our sins.

"But, God has provided a wonderful remedy (**God's Remedy**) for our terrible dilemma. Let's look at Romans 5:8. [The verse is read aloud.] It is incredible, but Christ died in our place. He took the penalty for our sins on Himself on the cross.

"Now let's look at Ephesians 2:8-9. [The verses are read aloud.] Many people believe that God is keeping score of what we do right and what we do wrong and that when we die, God adds up the scores. If we have done more good than bad, we get to go into Heaven. You can see in Ephesians 2:8-9 that eternal life is a gift. Romans 6:23, that we looked at earlier, also said that eternal life is a gift. We can't work for a gift. If we work for it, then it is wages. You can see here in Ephesians 2 that salvation and eternal life do not come to us through our good deeds.

"Finally, we need to look at **Our Response**. Eternal life is a free gift, but each person must reach out and receive or accept that free gift — to embrace it by faith. Everybody doesn't automatically have the gift of eternal life. But, we can ask for eternal life based on an understanding of Christ's death on the cross for us.

"Let's read John 1:12. [The verse is read aloud.] John 1:12 says that when anyone reaches out and receives Christ into his or her heart (or inner life) that person becomes a child of God in a new and very special way.

"Let's look at Romans 10:9-10. [The verses are read aloud.] Do you believe the things we've seen in these several verses? Do you believe them down in your heart as it says here in Romans 10? God would love to hear you say to Him out loud that you believe them. I suggest that in a few minutes we say a simple prayer to God and let Him know that you believe these things and that you want Christ to come into the center of your life.

"But, let's look at one final **summary** verse. It's wonderful! Look at John 5:24. [The verse is read aloud.] You see it says that if a person hears these things we're talking about and if that person genuinely believes them in his or her heart, three things happen. First, that person has eternal life right then and there. Second, that person will never have to stand before God, as Judge, and face severe consequences. And, third, that person passes from the eternal death side over to the eternal life side.

"I suggest that we have a 'make sure prayer' — that we say a prayer to God and let Him hear from your own lips that you understand and believe what Christ has done for you. Then ask Christ to come into your heart and life and to apply His death on the cross for you — for the forgiveness of your sins. Ask Him to take over your life, to give you the gift of eternal life, and to help you become all He wants you to be and to help you do whatever He wants you to do. Tell Him you are turning away from your sins and that you want to live a new life, close to Him as He helps you do that. Thank Him for Jesus Christ. Finish by saying 'Amen.'"

Keep in mind that this is a sample. When you explain The Bridge, do it in a way that is clear and logical to you. Both the contents of the presentation and the suggested prayer are highly adaptable. But, be sure your explanation of The Bridge and the prayer of commitment contain all the essential elements.

Come to session 8 ready to **draw out The Bridge outline** — everything that is visual. Then, in the following weeks you will **present The Bridge in a "lecture"** form as illustrated in the sample given above.

Make brief notes you can refer to as you practice the outline. Also make notes you can use during your practice for the lecture presentations. Keep the visual picture in mind. It will help you keep the sequence in order.

As a part of this course you have memorized several of the verses you will use in The Bridge. But, when you use The Bridge it is better for you to have the verses read rather than quoting them. (You may choose to use or not use 1 Peter 3:18. It is not essential to a strong presentation of The Bridge.)

ASSIGNMENT FOR SESSION 8:

1. Scripture Memory: Review all the verses memorized in Book 3.
2. Quiet Time: Continue your Bible reading, marking, and recording.
3. Bible Study: Complete the Bible study, "Integrity in Living" (pages 66-71).
4. Evangelism:
   a. Come to class prepared to give your personal testimony with or without notes in less than four minutes.
   b. Prepare to draw the outline (verses and main points) of *The Bridge Illustration* for another member of the class.

SESSION 8

OUTLINE OF THIS SESSION:
1. Break into verse review groups and work on getting anything signed that you can on your *Completion Record.*
2. Share some quiet time thoughts from your *Bible Reading Highlights Record.*
3. Have two or three people give a personal testimony with or without notes in less than four minutes.
4. Discuss the progress you are making with nonChristians.
5. Break into groups of two and take turns presenting *The Bridge Illustration* outline.
6. Discuss the Bible study, "Integrity in Living" (pages 66-71).
7. Read the "Assignment for Session 9" (page 71).
8. Close in prayer.

INTEGRITY IN LIVING

We must each deal daily with issues of right versus wrong—good versus evil. When struggling with these issues, we often tend to rationalize our behavior and compromise God's standards of integrity. Often these sins are explained away or ignored. These are the "vices of the virtuous"—sins which may have become accepted as the normal standard. But we must not allow any compromise with sin to infiltrate our lives.

THINK ABOUT:
How do you feel about "little white lies"?

THE STRUGGLE FOR INTEGRITY
Integrity is defined as being of sound moral principle; consistently upright, honest, and sincere.

1. Describe the natural condition of our hearts. Jeremiah 17:9 _____

_____

_____

_____

2. What are some of the ways we can be deceived?

    James 1:22 _____

    1 John 1:8 _____

    Romans 16:17-18 _____

    Ephesians 4:14 _____

    2 Corinthians 11:3-4 _____

3. Saul, the first king of Israel, is a good example of a man who lacked personal integrity. Read 1 Samuel 15:1-23.
    a. What was Saul commanded to do? Verses 1-3 _____

    _____

    _____

    _____

    b. What did he do? Verse 9 _____

    _____

    _____

    _____

    c. How did he try to justify his disobedience? Verses 13-21 _____

    _____

    _____

    _____

    d. How did God view the situation? Verses 22-23 _____

    _____

    _____

    _____

    _____

4. Hypocrites pretend to be what they are not. Study Mark 7:6-8, then list what Jesus says about hypocrites and give an example of each.

THE HYPOCRITE	EXAMPLE
_____	_____
_____	_____
_____	_____
_____	_____

LIVING A LIFE OF INTEGRITY

5. Read 1 Thessalonians 2:3-11.
   How did the apostle Paul demonstrate a life of integrity?
   a. By speech _____

   _____

   b. By deed _____

   _____

   c. Through motives _____

   _____

6. Read 1 Timothy 3:1-9.
   a. Which qualities required of a person seeking church office have to do with integrity? _____

   _____

   b. Are these qualities only for church leaders, or for everyone to attain? Explain your answer. _____

   _____

7. List the qualities of a person of integrity from Psalm 15:1-5. _____

   _____

   _____

Which of these qualities do you think are most violated among the people
with whom you associate? Consider both Christians and nonChristians.

_____

_____

_____

_____

8. Integrity needs to be displayed in all aspects of our lives.
   a. List below some of the areas where integrity tends to be neglected.

   Romans 13:6-7 _____

   Ephesians 5:22 _____

   Ephesians 5:25 _____

   Ephesians 6:1,2 _____

   Colossians 3:23-24 _____

   1 Peter 2:13-14 _____

   b. Is there ever a time when integrity toward God would override our com-
      mitment to these areas of responsibility? See Acts 4:18-20 and 5:27-29.

      _____

      _____

      _____

THE CONSCIENCE—AN AID TO INTEGRITY
   9. How does the dictionary define "conscience"? _____

      _____

      _____

      _____

10. From the following passages, describe the conscience.

   1 Corinthians 8:7-12 _____

   1 Timothy 3:9_____

   1 Timothy 4:2_____

   Titus 1:15 _____

   Hebrews 10:22 _____

   1 Peter 3:16,21 _____

11. Read Acts 24:16.

   a. What were Paul's objectives regarding his conscience? _____

_____

_____

_____

_____

   b. How can we develop or maintain this kind of conscience?

   Toward God _____

_____

   Toward Man _____

_____

SUMMARY

Review the chapter subtopics and write your own summary of each section.

The Struggle for Integrity

_____

_____

_____

_____

_____

_____

_____

Living a Life of Integrity

_____

_____

_____

_____

_____

_____

_____

_____

The Conscience—An Aid to Integrity

_____

_____

_____

_____

_____

_____

_____

_____

ASSIGNMENT FOR SESSION 9:
1. Scripture Memory: Work on any requirements not yet completed.
2. Quiet Time: Continue your Bible reading, marking, and recording.
3. Evangelism:
    a. Come to class prepared to give your personal testimony with or without notes in less than four minutes.
    b. Prepare to draw out and explain _The Bridge Illustration_ to another member of the class. (This is "Lecture Presentation 1")
4. Other:
    a. Study and complete "Verse Analysis of Matthew 6:33" (pages 72-75).
    b. Study and complete "Priorities—Part 1" (pages 76-80).

SESSION 9

OUTLINE OF THIS SESSION:
1. Break into review groups and work on getting anything signed that you can on your *Completion Record*.
2. Share some quiet time thoughts from your *Bible Reading Highlights Record*.
3. In groups of two, take turns drawing and explaining *The Bridge Illustration*.
4. Have two or three people give a personal testimony with or without notes in less than four minutes.
5. Discuss "Verse Analysis of Matthew 6:33" (pages 72-75).
6. Discuss "Priorities—Part 1" (pages 76-80).
7. Read the "Assignment for Session 10" (page 80).
8. Close in prayer regarding your priorities.

Verse Analysis of Matthew 6:33
Preparation for a Discussion on Priorities

This study is foundational for the discussion on priorities in sessions 9-10. After reading the context of Matthew 6:33 aloud twice, you will take these steps to analyze it:

1. Paraphrase the verse
2. Study the context
3. Find cross-references
4. Write down real or potential problems
5. Make a personal application

❑ I have read Matthew 6:19-34 aloud twice. (Check when completed.)

1. PARAPHRASE
Paraphrase Matthew 6:33 in your own words. Consult the translations in the box on the following page to stimulate your thinking.

"But seek first his kingdom and his righteousness, and all these things will be given to you as well."

"But seek first the kingdom of God and His righteousness, and all these things shall be added to you" (NKJV).

"But seek first His kingdom and His righteousness; and all these things shall be added to you" (NASB).

"Set your hearts on his kingdom first, and on his righteousness, and all these other things will be given you as well" (JB).

"But seek for (aim at and strive after) first of all His kingdom, and His righteousness [His way of doing and being right], and then all these things taken together will be given you besides" (AMP).

---

2. CONTEXT

Summarize the key thoughts in Matthew 6:25-32 and 6:34. Do *not* include verse 33. _____

_____

_____

_____

_____

_____

_____

_____

_____

3. CROSS-REFERENCES

What is the thought contained in the following verses that is similar to Matthew 6:33?

Deuteronomy 28:2 _____

_____

2 Chronicles 26:5 _____

_____

2 Chronicles 31:20-21 _____

_____

_____

Psalm 84:11 _____

_____

4. PROBLEMS

a. Define *righteousness* and *kingdom of God* in the following spaces. You will want to use a dictionary, Bible dictionary, encyclopedia, or commentary in preparing your definitions. You may need to check with your church library or with a friend who has these resource books.

Righteousness _____

_____

_____

_____

_____

_____

Kingdom of God _____

_____

_____

_____

_____

_____

b. What does the word *seek* imply? _____

_____

_____

_____

c. This verse opens with the word *but*. As you compare verse 33 with verses 31-32, what contrast does the word *but* imply? _____

_____

_____

_____

_____

5. APPLICATION

What is one application of Matthew 6:33 that you can make to your own life?

_____

_____

_____

_____

_____

_____

_____

_____

_____

Priorities—Part 1

Priorities have to do with order and importance. A priority list includes things in the order of their importance.

Why do we feel one thing is more important than another? It depends on what we want and what we would like to accomplish—what our goals and desires are. We all have goals and desires and these influence our choices.

A Christian's priorities should be based on God's will for his or her life as revealed in the Scriptures. Jesus Christ gave us the injunction, "But seek first his kingdom and his righteousness" (Matthew 6:33). That which pertains to God's kingdom has priority over our physical needs according to the context of the Sermon on the Mount.

To have the right priorities, we must have the right goals. From the following passages, write the goals and desires these godly men had or exhorted others to have.

- David (Psalm 27:4)_____

    _____

- Joshua (Joshua 24:15)_____

    _____

- Jesus (John 4:34)_____

    _____

- Paul (Romans 12:2)_____

    _____

- Paul (Colossians 1:28-29)_____

    _____

- John (3 John 4)_____

    _____

As committed Christians, we should "imitate their faith."

Remember your leaders, who spoke the word of God to you. Consider the outcome of their way of life and imitate their faith.

—Hebrews 13:7

GOALS

The goals for our lives, on which our priorities should be based, can be divided into two areas: (1) what we are to *be*—growing in Christlikeness (Romans 8:29) and (2) what we are to *do*—grow in effective service (Galatians 6:9-10).

Christlikeness

Make a list of the characteristics of Christlikeness from the following passages (use a translation, not a paraphrase):

GALATIANS 5:22-23	MATTHEW 5:3-10
1. _____	1. _____
2. _____	2. _____
3. _____	3. _____
4. _____	4. _____
5. _____	5. _____
6. _____	6. _____
7. _____	7. _____
8. _____	8. _____
9. _____	

Make a list of what you feel are the five most important characteristics of Christlikeness from the preceding lists:

1. _____   4. _____

2. _____   5. _____

3. _____

Serving

Serving means helping at the point of need. This may mean offering aid or advice; it could also mean admonishing a friend, sharing the gospel, or helping someone memorize Scripture.

There are many ways in which we may serve others. Match some principles with the Scripture references:

_____ Mark 9:41   1. Doing humble tasks for God's children

_____ John 13:14-16   2. Caring for widows

_____ Acts 6:1-3   3. Helping meet material or financial needs

_____ Ephesians 4:12   4. Praying for others

_____ Ephesians 6:5-7   5. Building up other Christians

_____ Colossians 4:12   6. Being thorough and hardworking on the job

_____ 1 Timothy 5:17   7. Giving a drink of cold water

_____ 1 John 3:17-18   8. Preaching and teaching the Word of God

The greatest service you can render to people is to bring them into a right relationship with Jesus Christ. This could be helping someone come to salvation in Christ or ministering to the spiritual development of a Christian.

"Seeking the kingdom of God first" has to do with glorifying God in the lives of individuals. So your highest concern in serving Christ is to minister to spiritual needs, and then to other needs which people have. At times it might be necessary to minister to the material or physical needs before you can minister to spiritual needs.

GUIDELINES FOR SETTING AND APPLYING PRIORITIES

1. **Make responsible choices.** Many of life's choices are already made for us: by Scripture (God), parents, government, and physical limitations. But whenever we have options, we are responsible to make choices. Slaves had little power of choice, yet in the first century the gospel spread rapidly among them.

2. **Be decisive.** One of the greatest hindrances to doing God's will is a lack of planning. Most of us have about 40 unplanned hours a week where we must choose how we will use that time. Take time to plan prayerfully with Matthew 6:33 as your guide. For example, plan how you will use a free evening or a Saturday or Sunday afternoon.

3. **Plan ahead.** The following approach can sharpen your effectiveness:
   a. Make one list of things you need to do, and another list of things you want to do.
   b. Pray for sensitivity from the Holy Spirit as you evaluate your lists.
   c. Number the items (1, 2, 3, and so on) in the order of their importance.
   d. Do item 1. Then do item 2, and so on through your list. Your list will need to be revised periodically because of a steady stream of new demands and opportunities. Many people make a new list every morning.

4. **Persevere.** Determination and perseverance are two necessary ingredients for living according to priorities. The flesh will often rebel against doing what you should do. Paul said, "I beat my body and make it my slave"(1 Corinthians 9:27). In other words, he is saying, "I make it do what it should do, not what it wants to do."

5. **Acknowledge dependence on God.** While we acknowledge that determination and perseverance are necessary ingredients for living by priorities, we must also acknowledge that God gives blessing and grace so that our efforts really count (see 2 Corinthians 3:5; John 15:5; Zechariah 4:6). Depend on God's enablement!

6. **Be adaptable.** In the book of James we are taught that when we have made our plans, we must learn to say, "If the Lord wills, we will carry them out" (see James 4:13-16). God sometimes has plans for us of which we are unaware. His thoughts are higher than our thoughts (see Isaiah 55:9), so don't get "bent out of shape" when interruptions come, but rather submit to God with thanksgiving in all your circumstances (see Romans 8:28; Psalm 115:3).

7. **Don't be easily swayed.** Some people will try to control our lives. At one point in his ministry people were trying to make plans for Christ (see Luke 4:42-44), but He would not submit to them. He said He had to do what His Father sent Him to do. Knowing what God wants you to do will enable you to discern when to submit to the desires of well-meaning people and when graciously to say "no."

8. **Review your goals.** In order to improve in making right choices based on God's goals for our lives, we must often reconsider these goals and evaluate whether we are making right choices. Human nature tends to lead us away from our goals. A half day alone with God regularly is an excellent activity for helping maintain motivation and a sense of priority.

9. **Prioritize.** Working by priority does not mean you will get everything done that you would like to. It does mean you will get the most important things done. Jesus said, "I have brought you [God the Father] glory on earth by completing the work you gave me to do" (John 17:4). Yet, there was much more He could have done. Let us learn from Jesus' example— live by God's priorities for our lives and commit to Him the things we are unable to do.

CONCLUSION

Sometimes priorities are based on selfish desires. The flesh tends to make it difficult for us to relate our priorities to God's plan for our lives because that involves sacrifice.

Do you want God to be "first" in your life? Then working on His purposes and priorities will be a lifelong process. Don't be discouraged when you fail, but instead make periodic evaluations, such as regularly spending a half day in prayer and planning. Remember the Lord's admonition, "Seek FIRST His Kingdom!"

ASSIGNMENT FOR SESSION 10:

1. Scripture Memory: Continue reviewing your verses and work on any requirements not yet completed.
2. Quiet Time: Continue your Bible reading, marking, and recording.
3. Evangelism:
   a. Come to class prepared to give your personal testimony with or without notes in less than four minutes.
   b. In groups of two, draw and explain The Bridge to each other. (This is "Lecture Presentation 2.")
4. Other: Read and be prepared to discuss "Priorities—Part 2" (pages 81-86).

SESSION 10

OUTLINE OF THIS SESSION:
1. Break into verse review groups and work on getting anything signed that you can on your *Completion Record.*
2. Share some quiet time thoughts from your *Bible Reading Highlights Record.*
3. Have two or three people give a personal testimony with or without notes in less than four minutes.
4. In groups of two, draw and explain *The Bridge Illustration* to each other.
5. Discuss "Priorities—Part 2" (pages 81-86).
6. Read the "Assignment for Session 11" (page 86).
7. Close in prayer.

Priorities—Part 2

THE PRIORITY OF GOD

"An unmarried man is concerned about the Lords' affairs—how he can please the Lord. But a married man is concerned about the affairs of this world—how he can please his wife" (1 Corinthians 7:32-33).

For every Christian man or woman, whether single or married, God must be the first priority. E. M. Bounds' classic statement, "To be little with God is to be little for God," captures the idea of this priority. We spend time with God because He greatly desires our fellowship. He longs to be with us, for we are "the kind of worshipers the Father seeks" (John 4:23). In His presence we grow in godliness, and the reality of our relationship with God becomes apparent to those around us. "When they saw the courage of Peter and John and realized that they were unschooled, ordinary men, they were astonished and they took note that these men had been with Jesus" (Acts 4:13).

Occasionally larger blocks of time with God should supplement your regular devotional times. Become strong in your grasp of the Word of God through Scripture memory and Bible study. Pray regularly that God will give you wisdom in applying the Word to your life. If you have a grasp on the great truths of the Bible, you will frequently find yourself in places of effective ministry. In time, your life will touch the lives of many.

The triangle diagram shows that the closer two individuals are to God, the closer they will be to each other. This is true between husband and wife, between parent and child—between any two Christians. Therefore, as you pursue God Himself, you will reap relational benefits

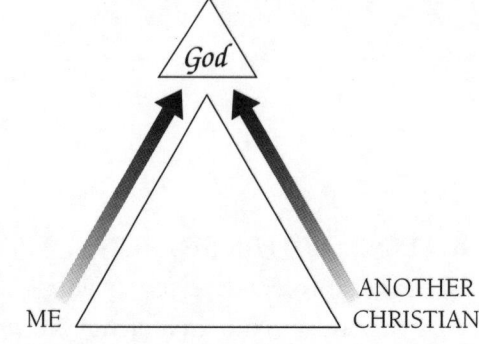

as well as personal benefits. Put your walk with God first! "As for me, it is good to be near God. I have made the Sovereign LORD my refuge" (Psalm 73:28). "The LORD is near to all who call on him, to all who call on him in truth. He fulfills the desires of those who fear him . . ." (Psalm 145:18-19).

CIRCLES OF PRIORITY

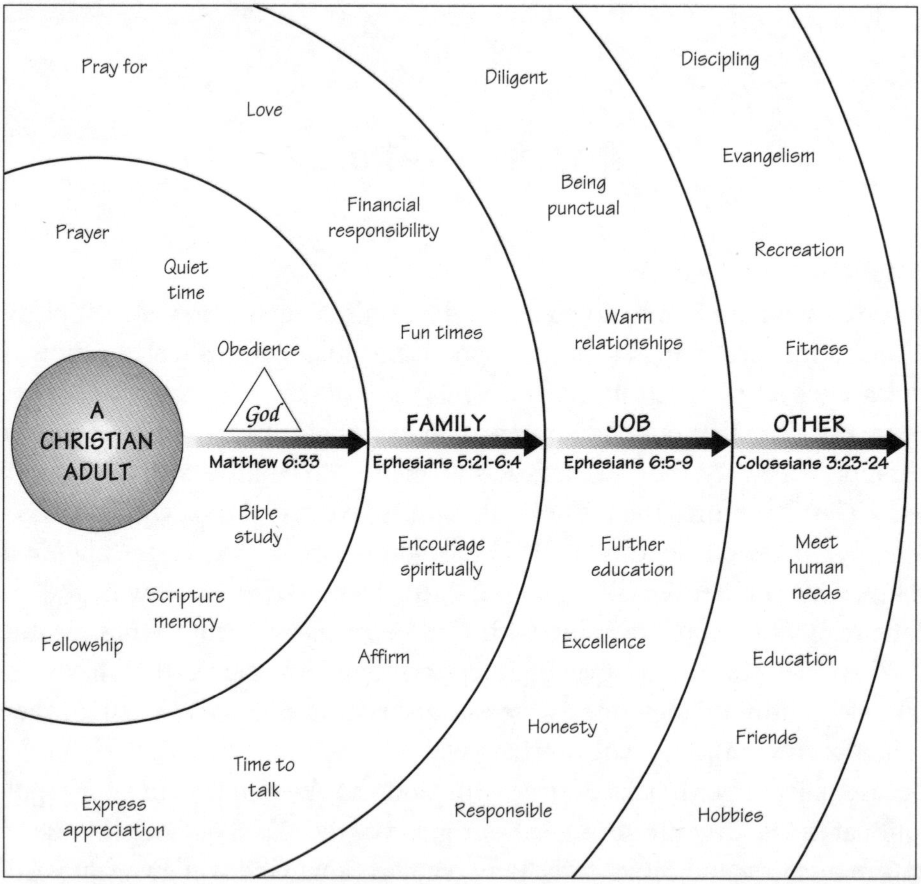

Pray for	Diligent	Discipling
Love		
Prayer	Being punctual	Evangelism
Financial responsibility		Recreation
Quiet time		
Obedience	Fun times	Warm relationships	Fitness

A CHRISTIAN ADULT → *God* / Matthew 6:33 → **FAMILY** / Ephesians 5:21-6:4 → **JOB** / Ephesians 6:5-9 → **OTHER** / Colossians 3:23-24

Bible study

Scripture memory

Fellowship

Express appreciation

Time to talk

Affirm

Encourage spiritually

Responsible

Further education

Excellence

Honesty

Meet human needs

Education

Friends

Hobbies

CIRCLES OF PRIORITY

The previous illustration, "Circles of Priority," is a visual representation of our common areas of responsibility in life. The inner circles are of higher priority. Yet, you will want to work toward balance in all areas of life right from the beginning.

God has given each of us basic responsibilities we must not neglect. Ultimately you will determine in your own heart and mind what is a priority for you in a given week or on a given day. We must give priority tasks and relationships extra weight when planning and scheduling our time.

Before we can be significantly effective for Christ, we must spend consistent, meaningful time with God. He is to be our first priority (Matthew 6:33). "He has showed you, O man, what is good. And what does the LORD require of you? To act justly and to love mercy and to walk humbly with your God" (Micah 6:8).

THE PRIORITY OF FAMILY

The best springboard for a great influence for Christ in the lives of many people may be simply sharing the biblical principles that work in your marriage or in raising your children.

Credibility in the family must precede expansion of spiritual influence. "If anyone does not know how to manage his own family, how can he take care of God's church?" (1 Timothy 3:5) Not that you must have everything in order in every dimension of your family life, but you must give a high priority to getting your own house in order. Your home will become either a springboard to greater ministry or a painful hindrance to all you do.

"For I have chosen him, so that he will direct his children and his household after him to keep the way of the LORD by doing what is right and just, so that the LORD will bring about for Abraham what he has promised him" (Genesis 18:19). Because of Abraham's faithfulness in the management of his family, God was able to prosper him in other ways.

Husband or Wife

Having a close vital relationship with God increases the probability of having a close vital relationship with your spouse. And having a good relationship in your marriage increases the probability of having a good relationship with your child. Priority does not imply neglect. It implies emphasis. Continue to work on your marriage.

Wives. Are you praying for your husband? Are you helping him to become more and more the leader and decision-maker he should be? Are you adapting to him? Are you a student of your husband, learning his moods, likes and dislikes, and strengths and weaknesses? Do you support and encourage him in what he feels led to pursue in life?

Husbands. Are you praying for your wife? Are you lifting your share of the load in household responsibilities and with your children? Have you read a book, listened to a tape, or seen a Christian film lately to sharpen your parenting skills? Are you and your wife thinking and planning together? Would your wife say you talk and pray together often enough? How often do you say, "Thank you?" Are you helping to meet your wife's spiritual, physical, and emotional needs as well as the financial ones?

You will have your greatest effectiveness in furthering the purposes of God in the world if you put your relationship to God first and give your spouse the strong second priority.

Children

Whether you are married or find yourself in the situation of being a single parent, you will agree that your children are both an unbelievable blessing and an incredible responsibility. However, we live in a most opportune time in history. The Christian sector has a proliferation of books, tapes, and seminars on how to raise children. Many pastors or Christian counselors are experienced and trained to assist us through some of the more difficult struggles. We must allow time to acquire the necessary knowledge and skills and have the courage to seek sound advice or counseling when needed.

We want to avoid bypassing our children for "the ministry." We may find that we have not prepared our children for the opportunities and difficulties of life or helped them become disciples of Jesus Christ. When children are younger we may need to decrease our involvement in ministry—realizing that our own children represent a very high ministry priority.

Single Adults

If you are a single adult, you have special benefits and advantages that enable you to make a significant contribution to what God desires to accomplish in the world today.

A large segment of the adult population is single. Single people are often more mobile and flexible in where they can live and what they can do. They have more time for Bible intake and spiritual growth than many married people. They usually are less hindered in reaching out to others in pursuing spiritual and general personal development. This, however, is not true for a single parent with the important opportunity and responsibility of caring for children.

How much further education should you pursue? How much time should you spend with friends, neighbors, or roommates? What kind of ministry load can you carry and still have time off and avoid excessive pressure and stress? God can lead you, so make these issues a matter of prayer and give adequate time for planning and evaluation.

Invest your single life wisely! Become all that God wants you to be and use the leverage of your situation to make your impact for Christ. God may lead you to get married one day, or He may best be able to work in and through you if you remain single. Your responsibility is to follow Christ wholeheartedly and to trust Him for a fulfilling and significant future.

THE PRIORITY OF JOB

Your secular job may take up many hours each week. But it is a place where you can use your God-given skills and abilities. It supplies funds that can be invested to further the cause of Jesus Christ, as well as finances to meet your personal and family needs.

The job can also be your point of contact and friendship with a number of nonChristians who may come to Christ and become disciples. You should do your ministering, of course, without using "company time." Your work on the job needs to be done "heartily as to the Lord" (Colossians 3:23), and so provide an open door for ministry as well as a source of provision and a sense of accomplishment.

THE PRIORITY OF CHURCH

Being a part of a local assembly of believers is most important! It is a place for both spiritual intake and ministry output.

Teaching a class of adults, young people, or children can be both a ministry and a context within which you can grow in your ability to motivate others and to communicate biblical truth clearly.

There are numerous opportunities to grow and minister. Pray for God's leading. Plan to be both taking in and giving out as you meet with other believers each week.

MINISTRY AND OTHER PRIORITIES

In Books 1-3 in *The New 2:7 Series*, there has been a persistent emphasis on the importance of relating to nonChristians, identifying with Christ, and then sharing your testimony and/or the gospel. Ministry has to be a solid part of the lifestyle of every believer if we hope to ever impact the world significantly for Christ. An increasing number of biblically sound churches are seeing the importance of ministering to physical and emotional as well as spiritual needs. There are limitless possibilities of ministry for every lay person. Some of the finest traditional and innovative ministries are being carried out by people who are *not* on the staff of a local church. They are "regular" Christian people with a job and perhaps a home and family. Plan to invest a portion of your energies in spreading the gospel, helping people become disciples, and meeting human needs.

Are you reading books, listening to tapes, and enjoying a hobby? These are activities that can help make us sharper and more interesting to be around. Could further education perhaps help make you more effective in your job? Are you attending Christian or job-related seminars and conferences when they are available? We don't want to hit a plateau in life somewhere in our 30s, 40s, or beyond.

Are you getting adequate exercise and sufficient time for rest and recreation? We need to give adequate attention to the care and welfare of our bodies and emotions as well as to our spiritual lives and ministries.

ASSIGNMENT FOR SESSION 11:

1. Scripture Memory: Work on getting any final memory requirements completed.
2. Quiet Time: Continue your Bible reading, marking, and recording.
3. Bible Study: Complete the Bible study, "Character in Action" (pages 87-93).

SESSION 11

OUTLINE OF THIS SESSION:
1. Break into verse review groups, and get anything signed that you can on your *Completion Record.*
2. Share some quiet time thoughts from your *Bible Reading Highlights Record.*
3. Discuss the Bible study, "Character in Action" (pages 87-93).
4. Review what you have learned in *Bearing Fruit in God's Family* and the first two courses of *The 2:7 Series* by reading aloud "Keep On Keeping On" (pages 93-94).
5. Close in prayer.

CHARACTER IN ACTION

A Christian is not immune to the harsh realities of human life. Sickness, sorrow, death, and other forms of pain and suffering are experienced by all people. But for a Christian, trials and suffering carry with them the promise of God's loving presence and sovereign purpose in shaping the inner qualities of life.

> **THINK ABOUT:**
> Why do you think God allows Christians to experience trials and suffering?

GOD'S ULTIMATE CONTROL
1. The Scriptures tell us that God is all-powerful (omnipotent), all-knowing (omniscient), and everywhere present (omnipresent).
   a. Read Psalm 139:1-16 and summarize God's involvement with you in the following areas:
   God's knowledge of me. Verses 1-6 _____

   _____

   _____

   _____

God's presence with me. Verses 7-12 _____

_____

_____

_____

God's development of me. Verses 13-16 _____

_____

_____

_____

   b. What was the response of the psalmist to the knowledge of God's influ-
     ence in his life?
     Verses 17-18 _____

_____

     Verses 23-24 _____

_____

_____

  2. What do the following verses teach about God's perspective and purpose?
     Isaiah 45:5-7 _____

_____

     Isaiah 46:9-10 _____

_____

     Romans 8:28 _____

_____

TRIALS AND SUFFERING PRODUCE CHARACTER
  3. Read James 1:2-4,12.
     a. How should a person respond to trials? _____

_____

_____

     b. What are the results of properly responding to trials? _____

_____

_____

  4. In Romans 5:3-5, Paul says we are to exult (rejoice, glory) in our tribulations.
     a. What does tribulation produce in the Christian's life? _____

_____

_____

_____

b. Is it important that Paul mentioned these areas in a particular sequence? Why or why not?_____

_____

_____

5. How did the following men deal with adversity?

Joseph (Genesis 50:20) _____

_____

Job (Job 1:13-22) _____

_____

Shadrach, Meshach, Abednego (Daniel 3:13-18) _____

_____

The Apostles (Acts 5:40-42) _____

_____

Paul (Philippians 1:12-21) _____

_____

What impresses you most from these examples?_____

_____

_____

6. What are some of the reasons God tested the people of Israel? Deuteronomy 8:1-3,16 _____

_____

_____

RESPONSE TO TRIALS AND SUFFERING

7. Sometimes the suffering we go through is a result of God's discipline. Read Hebrews 12:4-11.
a. Why does God discipline us?_____

_____

_____

_____

b. What are the results of God's discipline? _____

_____

_____

c. How do you think you can tell the difference between the discipline of
God and the attack of Satan? _____

_____

_____

8. Though trials and suffering are difficult at the time, what are some positive
aspects to consider?

Romans 8:18 _____

_____

2 Corinthians 1:3-4 _____

_____

1 Peter 5:10 _____

_____

Can you think of other positive aspects of suffering? _____

_____

_____

_____

9. Read Ephesians 5:20 and 1 Thessalonians 5:18.

a. How does God want us to respond to every situation (including trials and
suffering)? _____

_____

_____

b. Why is this response important? _____

_____

_____

_____

A person's response to problems determines his maturity level. Each crisis is an opportunity for victory or defeat.

PROBLEM ⟶ RESPONSE ⟶ VICTORY
OR
DEFEAT

10. Think back over a specific trial or suffering you have gone through and consider the questions below:

a. What was the trial or suffering? _____

_____

_____

_____

b. How did you respond to it? _____

_____

_____

_____

c. How could you have responded better? _____

_____

_____

_____

d. Did you thank God for the circumstance? _____

_____

_____

_____

e. How did God use it in your life? _____

_____

_____

_____

f. Have you been able to use it to comfort someone else? _____

_____

_____

_____

When God wants to drill a man
  And thrill a man
  And skill a man.
When God wants to mold a man
  To play the noblest part;
When He yearns with all His heart
  To create so great and bold a man
That all the world shall be amazed,
  Watch His methods, watch His ways!
How He ruthlessly perfects
  Whom He royally elects!
How He hammers him and hurts him,
  And with mighty blows converts him
Into trial shapes of clay which
  Only God understands;
While his tortured heart is crying
  And he lifts beseeching hands!
How He bends but never breaks
  When his good He undertakes;
How He uses whom he chooses
  And with every purpose fuses him;
By every act induces him
  To try His splendor out—
God knows what He's about!
                                    —Anonymous

SUMMARY

Review the chapter subtopics and write your own summary of each section.

God's Ultimate Control

_____

_____

_____

_____

_____

Trials and Suffering Produce Character

_____

_____

_____

_____

_____

Response to Trials and Suffering

_____

_____

_____

_____

_____

_____

Keep On Keeping On

WHAT YOU HAVE ACCOMPLISHED
Congratulations, you now have completed all three of the workbooks in *The New 2:7 Series*:

> —*Growing Strong in God's Family*
> —*Deepening Your Roots in God's Family*
> —*Bearing Fruit in God's Family*

Your diligence has brought you through significant steps in your growing as a true disciple of Jesus Christ. Your Christian life and ministry have been enhanced by:

- Regularity in Scripture memory—you have now memorized at least 17 verses.
- Regularity in your quiet time—you are reading Scripture with an eye for marking, recording, and responding back to God in prayer.
- Regularity in Bible study—you have completed 17 topical lessons in question-and-answer type Bible studies.
- Presentation of your personal testimony, which you have written out and are able to give in under four minutes.
- Learning to explain the gospel as you draw out *The Bridge Illustration*.
- Praying conversationally and knowing how to spend extended time with God in a half-day of prayer.

- Being confronted with, submitting to, and living under the lordship of Christ.
- Learning how to meditate on the Scriptures.
- Learning how to recognize and set priorities in your life.

FREE CERTIFICATE OF COMPLETION

Congratulations! You have persevered. You deserve to be recognized for work well done! As you reach this significant milestone, Church Discipleship Ministry of The Navigators would like you to have a certificate of completion. On our web site, www.navigators.org/cdm, there is a link to 2:7 Series Free Downloads. There you will find a certificate template signed by our National Director. We suggest you might want to print on parchment or other high quality paper available from most office supply stores.

The desire accomplished is sweet to the soul.

— Proverbs 13:19 (KJV)

USE WHAT YOU KNOW — CONTINUE TO LEARN AND GROW

Graduation from high school appropriately has been called "Commencement," meaning "a beginning" or "a start." There are young men and women in their 20s who are "old." There are seasoned citizens in their 60s who are "young." Plan to be learning and growing for a lifetime. Don't make it drudgery. Make it an adventure!

Put into practice what you have learned in *The New 2:7 Series*. Review your memory verses regularly. Plan to have a quiet time at least five times each week. That kind of consistency produces great personal dividends for your life.

Blessings and Godspeed!

Notes

PAGE	SOURCE
29	*Knight's Book of Illustrations* (Chicago: Moody Press, 1970).
30	J. Oswald Sanders, *Spiritual Leadership* (Chicago: Moody Press, 1967).
44	*Knight's Book of Illustrations* (Chicago: Moody Press, 1970).
48	*The Marriage Affair,* J. Allan Petersen, editor (Wheaton, Illinois: Tyndale House Publishers, 1971).

BIBLE READING HIGHLIGHTS RECORD

"Happy are those who keep My ways. Hear instruction and be wise, and do not refuse it. Happy is the man listening to Me, watching daily at My gates, keeping watch at My doorposts."

—**Proverbs 8:32-34**, (BERK)

*Translation*_____ *Year* _____

○ **Sunday** Date_____ All I read today _____
Best thing I marked today: *Reference:* _____
*Thought:*_____
_____
_____

How it impressed me: _____
_____
_____
_____
_____
_____
_____
_____

○ **Monday** Date_____ All I read today _____
Best thing I marked today: *Reference:* _____
*Thought:*_____
_____
_____

How it impressed me: _____
_____
_____
_____
_____
_____
_____
_____

○ **Tuesday** Date_____ All I read today_____
Best thing I marked today: *Reference:* _____
*Thought:*_____
_____
_____

How it impressed me: _____
_____
_____
_____
_____
_____
_____

○ **Wednesday** Date_____ All I read today_____
Best thing I marked today: *Reference:* _____
*Thought:*_____
_____
_____
_____

How it impressed me: _____
_____
_____
_____
_____
_____
_____
_____
_____
_____

○ **Thursday** Date_____ All I read today_____
Best thing I marked today: *Reference:* _____
*Thought:*_____
_____
_____

How it impressed me: _____
_____
_____
_____
_____
_____
_____
_____

○ **Friday** Date_____ All I read today_____
Best thing I marked today: *Reference:* _____
*Thought:*_____
_____
_____

How it impressed me: _____
_____
_____
_____
_____
_____
_____
_____

○ **Saturday** Date_____ All I read today_____
Best thing I marked today: *Reference:* _____
*Thought:*_____
_____
_____

How it impressed me: _____
_____
_____
_____
_____
_____
_____

BIBLE READING HIGHLIGHTS RECORD

"Happy are those who keep My ways. Hear instruction and be wise, and do not refuse it. Happy is the man listening to Me, watching daily at My gates, keeping watch at My doorposts."

—Proverbs 8:32-34, (BERK)

Translation_____ Year _____

○ **Sunday** Date_____ All I read today _____
Best thing I marked today: *Reference:* _____
*Thought:*_____
_____
_____
_____

How it impressed me: _____
_____
_____
_____
_____
_____
_____
_____

○ **Monday** Date_____ All I read today_____
Best thing I marked today: *Reference:* _____
*Thought:*_____
_____
_____
_____

How it impressed me: _____
_____
_____
_____
_____
_____
_____
_____
_____
_____

○ **Tuesday** Date_____ All I read today_____
Best thing I marked today: *Reference:* _____
*Thought:*_____
_____
_____

How it impressed me: _____
_____
_____
_____
_____
_____
_____
_____

○ **Wednesday** Date_____ All I read today_____
Best thing I marked today: *Reference:* _____
*Thought:*_____
_____
_____

How it impressed me: _____
_____
_____
_____
_____
_____
_____
_____
_____

○ **Thursday** Date_____ All I read today_____
Best thing I marked today: *Reference:* _____
*Thought:*_____
_____
_____
_____

How it impressed me: _____
_____
_____
_____
_____
_____
_____
_____

○ **Friday** Date _____ All I read today_____
Best thing I marked today: *Reference:* _____
*Thought:*_____
_____
_____
_____

How it impressed me: _____
_____
_____
_____
_____
_____
_____
_____
_____

○ **Saturday** Date_____ All I read today _____
Best thing I marked today: *Reference:* _____
*Thought:*_____
_____
_____

How it impressed me: _____
_____
_____
_____
_____
_____
_____

BIBLE READING HIGHLIGHTS RECORD

"Happy are those who keep My ways. Hear instruction and be wise, and do not refuse it. Happy is the man listening to Me, watching daily at My gates, keeping watch at My doorposts."

—**Proverbs 8:32-34**, (BERK)

*Translation*_____ *Year*_____

Sunday   Date_____ All I read today_____
Best thing I marked today: *Reference:*_____
*Thought:*_____
_____
_____
_____
How it impressed me: _____
_____
_____
_____
_____
_____
_____
_____
_____

Monday   Date_____ All I read today_____
Best thing I marked today: *Reference:*_____
*Thought:*_____
_____
_____
_____
How it impressed me: _____
_____
_____
_____
_____
_____
_____
_____
_____
_____

Tuesday   Date_____ All I read today_____
Best thing I marked today: *Reference:*_____
*Thought:*_____
_____
_____
_____
How it impressed me: _____
_____
_____
_____
_____
_____
_____
_____

Wednesday   Date_____ All I read today_____
Best thing I marked today: *Reference:*_____
*Thought:*_____
_____
_____
_____
How it impressed me: _____
_____
_____
_____
_____
_____
_____
_____
_____
_____
_____
_____

Thursday   Date_____ All I read today_____
Best thing I marked today: *Reference:*_____
*Thought:*_____
_____
_____
_____
How it impressed me: _____
_____
_____
_____
_____
_____
_____
_____
_____
_____

Friday   Date_____ All I read today_____
Best thing I marked today: *Reference:*_____
*Thought:*_____
_____
_____
_____
How it impressed me: _____
_____
_____
_____
_____
_____
_____
_____
_____

Saturday   Date_____ All I read today_____
Best thing I marked today: *Reference:*_____
*Thought:*_____
_____
_____
_____
How it impressed me: _____
_____
_____
_____
_____
_____

BIBLE READING HIGHLIGHTS RECORD

"Happy are those who keep My ways. Hear instruction and be wise, and do not refuse it. Happy is the man listening to Me, watching daily at My gates, keeping watch at My doorposts."

—Proverbs 8:32-34, (BERK)

Translation_____ Year _____

○ **Sunday**   Date_____ All I read today _____
Best thing I marked today: *Reference:* _____
*Thought:*_____
_____
_____
_____

How it impressed me: _____
_____
_____
_____
_____
_____
_____
_____

○ **Monday**   Date_____ All I read today_____
Best thing I marked today: *Reference:* _____
*Thought:*_____
_____
_____
_____

How it impressed me: _____
_____
_____
_____
_____
_____
_____
_____

○ **Tuesday**   Date_____ All I read today_____
Best thing I marked today: *Reference:* _____
*Thought:*_____
_____
_____

How it impressed me: _____
_____
_____
_____
_____
_____
_____
_____

○ **Wednesday** Date_____ All I read today_____
Best thing I marked today: *Reference:* _____
*Thought:*_____
_____
_____
_____

How it impressed me: _____
_____
_____
_____
_____
_____
_____
_____
_____

○ **Thursday**   Date_____ All I read today_____
Best thing I marked today: *Reference:* _____
*Thought:*_____
_____
_____
_____

How it impressed me: _____
_____
_____
_____
_____
_____
_____

○ **Friday**   Date_____ All I read today_____
Best thing I marked today: *Reference:* _____
*Thought:*_____
_____
_____

How it impressed me: _____
_____
_____
_____
_____
_____
_____
_____

○ **Saturday**   Date_____ All I read today_____
Best thing I marked today: *Reference:* _____
*Thought:*_____
_____
_____

How it impressed me: _____
_____
_____
_____
_____
_____

BIBLE READING HIGHLIGHTS RECORD

"Happy are those who keep My ways. Hear instruction and be wise, and do not refuse it. Happy is the man listening to Me, watching daily at My gates, keeping watch at My doorposts."

—**Proverbs 8:32-34**, (BERK)

Translation_____ Year _____

○ **Sunday** Date_____ All I read today _____
Best thing I marked today: *Reference:* _____
*Thought:*_____
_____
_____
How it impressed me: _____
_____
_____
_____
_____
_____
_____
_____

○ **Monday** Date_____ All I read today _____
Best thing I marked today: *Reference:* _____
*Thought:*_____
_____
_____
How it impressed me: _____
_____
_____
_____
_____
_____
_____
_____
_____

○ **Tuesday** Date_____ All I read today _____
Best thing I marked today: *Reference:* _____
*Thought:*_____
_____
How it impressed me: _____
_____
_____
_____
_____
_____

○ **Wednesday** Date_____ All I read today _____
Best thing I marked today: *Reference:* _____
*Thought:*_____
_____
_____
_____
How it impressed me: _____
_____
_____
_____
_____
_____
_____
_____
_____

○ **Thursday** Date_____ All I read today _____
Best thing I marked today: *Reference:* _____
*Thought:*_____
_____
_____
How it impressed me: _____
_____
_____
_____
_____
_____
_____

○ **Friday** Date _____ All I read today _____
Best thing I marked today: *Reference:* _____
*Thought:*_____
_____
_____
How it impressed me: _____
_____
_____
_____
_____
_____
_____
_____

○ **Saturday** Date_____ All I read today _____
Best thing I marked today: *Reference:* _____
*Thought:*_____
_____
How it impressed me: _____
_____
_____
_____
_____

BIBLE READING HIGHLIGHTS RECORD

"Happy are those who keep My ways. Hear instruction and be wise, and do not refuse it. Happy is the man listening to Me, watching daily at My gates, keeping watch at My doorposts."

—**Proverbs 8:32-34,** (BERK)

*Translation*_____ *Year* _____

○ Sunday   Date_____ All I read today _____
Best thing I marked today: *Reference:* _____
*Thought:*_____

How it impressed me: _____

○ Monday   Date_____ All I read today _____
Best thing I marked today: *Reference:* _____
*Thought:*_____

How it impressed me: _____

○ Tuesday   Date_____ All I read today_____
Best thing I marked today: *Reference:* _____
*Thought:*_____

How it impressed me: _____

○ Wednesday   Date_____ All I read today_____
Best thing I marked today: *Reference:* _____
*Thought:*_____

How it impressed me: _____

○ Thursday   Date_____ All I read today_____
Best thing I marked today: *Reference:* _____
*Thought:*_____

How it impressed me: _____

○ Friday   Date _____ All I read today_____
Best thing I marked today: *Reference:* _____
*Thought:*_____

How it impressed me: _____

○ Saturday   Date_____ All I read today _____
Best thing I marked today: *Reference:* _____
*Thought:*_____

How it impressed me: _____

BIBLE READING HIGHLIGHTS RECORD

"Happy are those who keep My ways. Hear instruction and be wise, and do not refuse it. Happy is the man listening to Me, watching daily at My gates, keeping watch at My doorposts."

—**Proverbs 8:32-34,** (BERK)

Translation_____ Year _____

Sunday   Date_____ All I read today _____
Best thing I marked today: *Reference:* _____
*Thought:*_____
_____
_____

How it impressed me: _____
_____
_____
_____
_____
_____
_____
_____

Monday   Date_____ All I read today _____
Best thing I marked today: *Reference:* _____
*Thought:*_____
_____
_____

How it impressed me: _____
_____
_____
_____
_____
_____
_____
_____

Tuesday   Date_____ All I read today _____
Best thing I marked today: *Reference:* _____
*Thought:*_____
_____
_____

How it impressed me: _____
_____
_____
_____
_____
_____
_____

Wednesday   Date_____ All I read today _____
Best thing I marked today: *Reference:* _____
*Thought:*_____
_____
_____
_____

How it impressed me: _____
_____
_____
_____
_____
_____
_____
_____
_____

Thursday   Date_____ All I read today _____
Best thing I marked today: *Reference:* _____
*Thought:*_____
_____
_____

How it impressed me: _____
_____
_____
_____
_____
_____
_____
_____

Friday   Date_____ All I read today _____
Best thing I marked today: *Reference:* _____
*Thought:*_____
_____
_____

How it impressed me: _____
_____
_____
_____
_____
_____
_____
_____

Saturday   Date_____ All I read today _____
Best thing I marked today: *Reference:* _____
*Thought:*_____
_____
_____

How it impressed me: _____
_____
_____
_____
_____
_____

BIBLE READING HIGHLIGHTS RECORD

"Happy are those who keep My ways. Hear instruction and be wise, and do not refuse it. Happy is the man listening to Me, watching daily at My gates, keeping watch at My doorposts."

—Proverbs 8:32-34, (BERK)

Translation _____ Year _____

○ **Sunday** Date _____ All I read today _____
Best thing I marked today: *Reference:* _____
Thought: _____
_____
_____

How it impressed me: _____
_____
_____
_____
_____
_____

○ **Monday** Date _____ All I read today _____
Best thing I marked today: *Reference:* _____
Thought: _____
_____
_____

How it impressed me: _____
_____
_____
_____
_____
_____
_____

○ **Tuesday** Date _____ All I read today _____
Best thing I marked today: *Reference:* _____
Thought: _____
_____
_____

How it impressed me: _____
_____
_____
_____
_____
_____

○ **Wednesday** Date _____ All I read today _____
Best thing I marked today: *Reference:* _____
Thought: _____
_____
_____

How it impressed me: _____
_____
_____
_____
_____
_____
_____
_____

○ **Thursday** Date _____ All I read today _____
Best thing I marked today: *Reference:* _____
Thought: _____
_____
_____

How it impressed me: _____
_____
_____
_____
_____
_____

○ **Friday** Date _____ All I read today _____
Best thing I marked today: *Reference:* _____
Thought: _____
_____
_____

How it impressed me: _____
_____
_____
_____
_____
_____

○ **Saturday** Date _____ All I read today _____
Best thing I marked today: *Reference:* _____
Thought: _____
_____
_____

How it impressed me: _____
_____
_____
_____
_____
_____

BIBLE READING HIGHLIGHTS RECORD

"Happy are those who keep My ways. Hear instruction and be wise, and do not refuse it. Happy is the man listening to Me, watching daily at My gates, keeping watch at My doorposts."

—**Proverbs 8:32-34**, (BERK)

*Translation*_____ *Year* _____

Sunday   Date_____ All I read today _____
Best thing I marked today: *Reference:* _____
*Thought:*_____
_____
_____

How it impressed me: _____
_____
_____
_____
_____
_____
_____
_____

Monday   Date_____ All I read today _____
Best thing I marked today: *Reference:* _____
*Thought:*_____
_____
_____
_____

How it impressed me: _____
_____
_____
_____
_____
_____
_____
_____
_____
_____

Tuesday   Date_____ All I read today_____
Best thing I marked today: *Reference:* _____
*Thought:*_____
_____
_____
_____

How it impressed me: _____
_____
_____
_____
_____
_____
_____

Wednesday   Date_____ All I read today_____
Best thing I marked today: *Reference:* _____
*Thought:*_____
_____
_____
_____

How it impressed me: _____
_____
_____
_____
_____
_____
_____
_____
_____

Thursday   Date_____ All I read today_____
Best thing I marked today: *Reference:* _____
*Thought:*_____
_____
_____

How it impressed me: _____
_____
_____
_____
_____
_____
_____
_____
_____
_____
_____

Friday   Date_____ All I read today_____
Best thing I marked today: *Reference:* _____
*Thought:*_____
_____
_____
_____

How it impressed me: _____
_____
_____
_____
_____
_____
_____
_____

Saturday   Date_____ All I read today_____
Best thing I marked today: *Reference:* _____
*Thought:*_____
_____
_____
_____

How it impressed me: _____
_____
_____
_____
_____
_____
_____

BIBLE READING HIGHLIGHTS RECORD

"Happy are those who keep My ways. Hear instruction and be wise, and do not refuse it. Happy is the man listening to Me, watching daily at My gates, keeping watch at My doorposts."

—Proverbs 8:32-34, (BERK)

*Translation*_____ *Year* _____

○ **Sunday**   Date_____ All I read today_____
Best thing I marked today: *Reference:* _____
*Thought:*_____
_____
_____

How it impressed me: _____
_____
_____
_____
_____
_____
_____
_____

○ **Monday**   Date_____ All I read today_____
Best thing I marked today: *Reference:* _____
*Thought:*_____
_____
_____

How it impressed me: _____
_____
_____
_____
_____
_____
_____
_____
_____

○ **Tuesday**   Date_____ All I read today_____
Best thing I marked today: *Reference:* _____
*Thought:*_____
_____
_____

How it impressed me: _____
_____
_____
_____
_____
_____
_____
_____

○ **Wednesday**   Date_____ All I read today_____
Best thing I marked today: *Reference:* _____
*Thought:*_____
_____
_____
_____
_____

How it impressed me: _____
_____
_____
_____
_____
_____
_____
_____
_____
_____

○ **Thursday**   Date_____ All I read today_____
Best thing I marked today: *Reference:* _____
*Thought:*_____
_____
_____

How it impressed me: _____
_____
_____
_____
_____
_____
_____
_____

○ **Friday**   Date_____ All I read today_____
Best thing I marked today: *Reference:* _____
*Thought:*_____
_____
_____

How it impressed me: _____
_____
_____
_____
_____
_____
_____
_____

○ **Saturday**   Date_____ All I read today_____
Best thing I marked today: *Reference:* _____
*Thought:*_____
_____
_____

How it impressed me: _____
_____
_____
_____
_____
_____
_____

BIBLE READING HIGHLIGHTS RECORD

"Happy are those who keep My ways. Hear instruction and be wise, and do not refuse it. Happy is the man listening to Me, watching daily at My gates, keeping watch at My doorposts."

—**Proverbs 8:32-34,** (BERK)

Translation _____ *Year* _____

○ **Sunday** Date _____ All I read today _____
Best thing I marked today: *Reference:* _____
Thought: _____
_____
_____

How it impressed me: _____
_____
_____
_____
_____
_____

○ **Monday** Date _____ All I read today _____
Best thing I marked today: *Reference:* _____
Thought: _____
_____
_____

How it impressed me: _____
_____
_____
_____
_____
_____

○ **Tuesday** Date _____ All I read today _____
Best thing I marked today: *Reference:* _____
Thought: _____
_____
_____

How it impressed me: _____
_____
_____
_____
_____
_____

○ **Wednesday** Date _____ All I read today _____
Best thing I marked today: *Reference:* _____
Thought: _____
_____
_____

How it impressed me: _____
_____
_____
_____
_____
_____
_____

○ **Thursday** Date _____ All I read today _____
Best thing I marked today: *Reference:* _____
Thought: _____
_____

How it impressed me: _____
_____
_____
_____
_____
_____

○ **Friday** Date _____ All I read today _____
Best thing I marked today: *Reference:* _____
Thought: _____
_____

How it impressed me: _____
_____
_____
_____
_____
_____

○ **Saturday** Date _____ All I read today _____
Best thing I marked today: *Reference:* _____
Thought: _____
_____

How it impressed me: _____
_____
_____
_____
_____

BIBLE READING HIGHLIGHTS RECORD

"Happy are those who keep My ways. Hear instruction and be wise, and do not refuse it. Happy is the man listening to Me, watching daily at My gates, keeping watch at My doorposts."

—**Proverbs 8:32-34,** (BERK)

Translation _____ Year _____

○ **Sunday** Date _____ All I read today _____
Best thing I marked today: *Reference:* _____
Thought: _____
_____

How it impressed me: _____
_____
_____
_____
_____
_____
_____

○ **Monday** Date _____ All I read today _____
Best thing I marked today: *Reference:* _____
Thought: _____
_____

How it impressed me: _____
_____
_____
_____
_____
_____
_____
_____

○ **Tuesday** Date _____ All I read today _____
Best thing I marked today: *Reference:* _____
Thought: _____
_____

How it impressed me: _____
_____
_____
_____
_____
_____
_____

○ **Wednesday** Date _____ All I read today _____
Best thing I marked today: *Reference:* _____
Thought: _____
_____
_____

How it impressed me: _____
_____
_____
_____
_____
_____
_____
_____
_____

○ **Thursday** Date _____ All I read today _____
Best thing I marked today: *Reference:* _____
Thought: _____

How it impressed me: _____
_____
_____
_____
_____
_____

○ **Friday** Date _____ All I read today _____
Best thing I marked today: *Reference:* _____
Thought: _____

How it impressed me: _____
_____
_____
_____
_____
_____
_____
_____

○ **Saturday** Date _____ All I read today _____
Best thing I marked today: *Reference:* _____
Thought: _____

How it impressed me: _____
_____
_____
_____
_____
_____
_____

BIBLE READING HIGHLIGHTS RECORD

"Happy are those who keep My ways. Hear instruction and be wise, and do not refuse it. Happy is the man listening to Me, watching daily at My gates, keeping watch at My doorposts."

—**Proverbs 8:32-34,** (BERK)

Translation_____ Year _____

○ **Sunday** Date_____ All I read today _____
Best thing I marked today: *Reference:* _____
*Thought:*_____
_____
_____
_____

How it impressed me: _____
_____
_____
_____
_____
_____
_____
_____

○ **Monday** Date_____ All I read today _____
Best thing I marked today: *Reference:* _____
*Thought:*_____
_____
_____

How it impressed me: _____
_____
_____
_____
_____
_____
_____
_____
_____
_____

○ **Tuesday** Date_____ All I read today_____
Best thing I marked today: *Reference:* _____
*Thought:*_____
_____
_____

How it impressed me: _____
_____
_____
_____
_____
_____

○ **Wednesday** Date_____ All I read today_____
Best thing I marked today: *Reference:* _____
*Thought:*_____
_____
_____
_____

How it impressed me: _____
_____
_____
_____
_____
_____
_____
_____
_____
_____

○ **Thursday** Date_____ All I read today_____
Best thing I marked today: *Reference:* _____
*Thought:*_____
_____
_____

How it impressed me: _____
_____
_____
_____
_____
_____
_____
_____

○ **Friday** Date_____ All I read today_____
Best thing I marked today: *Reference:* _____
*Thought:*_____
_____
_____

How it impressed me: _____
_____
_____
_____
_____
_____
_____
_____
_____

○ **Saturday** Date_____ All I read today_____
Best thing I marked today: *Reference:* _____
*Thought:*_____
_____
_____

How it impressed me: _____
_____
_____
_____
_____
_____
_____

BIBLE READING HIGHLIGHTS RECORD

"Happy are those who keep My ways. Hear instruction and be wise, and do not refuse it. Happy is the man listening to Me, watching daily at My gates, keeping watch at My doorposts."

—Proverbs 8:32-34, (BERK)

*Translation*_____ *Year*_____

Sunday   Date_____ All I read today_____
Best thing I marked today: *Reference:*_____
*Thought:*_____
_____
_____
_____
How it impressed me: _____
_____
_____
_____
_____
_____
_____

Monday   Date_____ All I read today_____
Best thing I marked today: *Reference:*_____
*Thought:*_____
_____
_____
How it impressed me: _____
_____
_____
_____
_____
_____
_____
_____
_____

Tuesday   Date_____ All I read today_____
Best thing I marked today: *Reference:*_____
*Thought:*_____
_____
_____
How it impressed me: _____
_____
_____
_____
_____
_____
_____
_____

Wednesday   Date_____ All I read today_____
Best thing I marked today: *Reference:*_____
*Thought:*_____
_____
_____
_____
_____
How it impressed me: _____
_____
_____
_____
_____
_____
_____
_____
_____

Thursday   Date_____ All I read today_____
Best thing I marked today: *Reference:*_____
*Thought:*_____
_____
_____
How it impressed me: _____
_____
_____
_____
_____
_____

Friday   Date_____ All I read today_____
Best thing I marked today: *Reference:*_____
*Thought:*_____
_____
_____
How it impressed me: _____
_____
_____
_____
_____
_____
_____
_____

Saturday   Date_____ All I read today_____
Best thing I marked today: *Reference:*_____
*Thought:*_____
_____
_____
How it impressed me: _____
_____
_____
_____
_____
_____
_____

Prayer Sheet

REQUEST	GOD'S ANSWER

Prayer Sheet

REQUEST	GOD'S ANSWER

CHURCH DISCIPLESHIP MINISTRY

CDM is a ministry of The Navigators that focuses on helping churches become more intentional in discipleship and outreach. CDM staff help pastors and church leaders develop an effective and personalized approach to accomplishing the Great Commission.

Through a nationwide network of staff, CDM works alongside the local church to build a strong structure for disciplemaking; one that is intentional. Six critical areas are core to an **Intentional Disciplemaking Church:**

- Mission

- Spiritual Maturity

- Outreach

- Leadership

- Small Groups

- Life-to-Life

CDM offers seminars, materials and coaching in these six areas for those interested in becoming an Intentional Disciplemaking Church. See our web page for further information on how CDM can help you.

www.navigators.org/cdm

or call our CDM Office at (719) 598-1212
or write to PO Box 6000, Colorado Springs, CO 80934

Discipleship Resources from Church Discipleship Ministry (CDM) and NavPress

☐ *Opening the Door*
- A user-friendly, seeker-oriented tool for helping people explore the Gospel message
- A tool kit full of tips on being an effective facilitator and recruiting new seekers
- Twenty Discovery Guides each using selected passages from the Gospel of Luke
- Each Discovery Guide can be photocopied and used for every new group or individual you intend to reach.
- Each Discovery Guide contains only one scripture reading and eight questions, allowing discussions to be completed in less than an hour over lunch or coffee.

Available from NavPress 1-800-366-7788

☐ *The Adventure of Discipling Others*
Just like Jesus, you can disciple believers, helping them grow spiritually and fulfill their unique niche in God's kingdom. With *The Adventure of Discipling Others,* anyone can mentor and love the process.

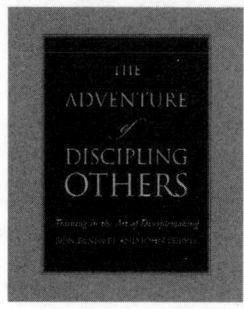

Available from NavPress 1-800-366-7788

The resources listed below are available from the Church Discipleship Ministry of The Navigators, at 1-719-598-1212 x2446:

☐ *Mission Master Plan (MMP)*
This vision-building working resource will help your church develop its own foundational elements of Purpose, Vision, Core Values, and Philosophy of Ministry. It also helps you create the bridge to your future through identifying: Critical Success Factors, Goals, Action Steps, and Vital Communication.

☐ *Leadership Assessment and Development (LAAD)*
This leadership consultation tool will assist your church leadership team in assessing how they are preparing leaders. It looks at your leadership profile and your development process and helps you assess and correct missing steps.

☐ *Authentic Evangelism Seminar (AES)*
This one-day training seminar helps a church develop the vision and strategy for intentional outreach. In addition to helping individuals become more confident in sharing their faith, it helps mobilize the whole church body toward using their gifting in reaching out to a broken world.

☐ *Discipling Others Seminar (New from CDM)*
This one-day seminar prepares disciples to disciple others. DOS will launch new disciplers into authentic discipling using either mentoring or small groups. This interactive seminar covers: The Vision for Making Disciples, Creating a Disciplemaking Environment, and Ministering Life-To-Life.